*You Really
Are
Responsible*

You Really Are Responsible

A guide to
self-empowerment
and improved relationships.

Tycho Photiou

There are many quotations included within this book. They are the words of wise men and women through the centuries, up to, and including, the present day. Many of the quotations are from various religious texts, particularly Buddhism and Christianity.

Some of the relatively modern sources are acknowledged in the bibliography. Whilst the publisher has made every effort to obtain permission for the quotations wherever appropriate, this may not have been possible in every case. We would therefore like to thank everyone who contributed to provide the wonderful and rich teachings that you will find within these pages, and accept our apologies if any modern sources have not been adequately acknowledged.

Where there is no attribution given to the quotations, they are the authors own.

Ocean Books
18 Pentrich Avenue,
Enfield,
Middlesex. EN1 4LZ.
Tel (0181) 350 9600

1st Edition - Published 1998

Printed in Great Britain by
St Edmundsbury Press Ltd, Bury St Edmunds, Suffolk.

AUTHORS NOTE:

The English Language has a weakness in that there is no word as yet to represent "he or she" in written language - the author would like to rectify this problem by making the following definitions:

They = he or she
Their = his or her
Them = him or her.

These definitions aren't really original, they are already used in this way considerably in spoken language - when a person speaks normally *they* very rarely say he or she, "they" is much more common. The author now feels that it is time to extend the use of these spoken abbreviations to the written form.

Contents

Preface

Andrea Photiou

This book will give the reader a comprehensive understanding of an alternative way through the maze of life. It explains that the power we need to change our circumstances, pursue our dreams and deal wisely with the many problems life tends to throw our way, is not found by only looking out for ourselves nor is it found in wishing and hoping things will change for the better. As you will see, the power lies within us and the influence we have over others and our surroundings. (It is only by caring for a subject that one can come to know it well and only by knowing it well can one become wiser and more confident in dealing with it).

We never know when misfortune will strike but when it does we have the choice to rise up with dignity and meet it face to face or we can lie down and become its victim. Self-empowerment is simply the ability to access the best of ourselves in order to access the best from life. Like the gentle drop of water that has the ability to reshape solid rock, we ourselves have the power to reshape our lives and circumstances. Not through force but through understanding and increased awareness and a genuine consideration towards ourselves and others. By employing kindness and integrity one can obtain the best of what is.

When was the last time that you woke up in the morning feeling genuinely happy to be who you are? It would be wonderful if we could feel like this every day, but often there is something inside us blocking the way and whilst it may be tempting to put the blame on to someone or something else, it is ourselves that we must work on to deal with these blocks. For everyone, life has a tendency to create problems, but sometimes we find ourselves in a permanent state of worry. In our distracted state we may lose sight of how good life can be and how good we are able to feel.

By following the simple yet inspiring philosophy within these pages the reader will come to understand that there really is an alternative way to deal with life using qualities which are natural and human. It is up to each individual to discover for themselves what they would wish to put into practice according to their own nature, and slowly come to realise just how effective a few simple changes can be in achieving the very best from life.

This book is a testament to the fact that the road to real freedom is always within your grasp. Through understanding your own nature and infinite potential you will inevitably find yourself embarking on a journey - an exciting journey that will last a lifetime.

Introduction

This book is all about self-empowerment. This has nothing to do with control or manipulation of others, it is all about developing the attitude "I am responsible for everything that happens to me in my life" as opposed to "I am the victim of my circumstances over which I have no control". The essence of the message within this book is that **we are not just helpless victims of circumstance, our life is a product of our consciousness and so as our consciousness changes, everything around us changes to correspond to this inner change.**

> *Blame what you will but nothing will change;*
> *it's something inside that you must rearrange.*
> ANDREA PHOTIOU

While you read this book try to have a good, hard look at yourself and think about the ways in which you might be responsible for the negative as well as the positive aspects of your life. But be careful - taking responsibility is not to be confused with "everything bad that happens to me is my own fault" since blame never gets us anywhere. Response-ability means the ability to respond, so even if you can't change a particular event, you can certainly change the way that you respond to it. As I explained in my previous book *you are what you think:*

> *It is the way we look at*
> *the scenery that needs changing,*
> *and not the scenery itself.*

Discovering
Self-empowerment

DISCOVERING
SELF-EMPOWERMENT

When we finally give up
the struggle to find fulfilment "out there",
we have nowhere to go but within.

SHAKTI GAWAIN

Although we always like to project the source of our discontentment and dissatisfaction onto something external the true cause is *nearly always* something internal and we only need to look within ourselves to find the answer to how we can be happier and more satisfied. **If we are dissatisfied and we change our job or our partner, this will only be of value if the change helps us to develop from within, otherwise the internal dissatisfaction will remain the same.**

You may say: "I am aware that the source of my discontentment is not material but comes from having nasty people around me who are always trying to make my life difficult." However, it is important to realise that, in general, **the people in your life interact with you according to *how you are*.** As your self-image improves, and as you become more open, helpful and loving, those "nasty" people will either change or disappear.

Everyone feels dissatisfied to some extent. These feelings of dissatisfaction or restlessness about life are good motivating factors to help us to develop by spurring us on to take the next step in life which might involve either changing our environmental situation or developing from within. However, the mistake that many people make is instead of using these feelings

7

of dissatisfaction as a spur to motivate themselves, they use the feelings to generate a whole series of complaints about what a bad deal in life they are getting. They cast the blame onto everyone and everything possible that is causing their misery and sadness, as if they have no part in the creation of their circumstances.

> *Your inner thoughts, beliefs and attitudes are causes,*
> *your external circumstances are effects.*

We are in a much healthier and more powerful position if we take responsibility for our own development and not assume that it depends on "the world out there". Progress in self-development comes when we look inside ourselves for the answers to our problems instead of trying to put the blame onto everyone and everything else.

> *Of course, fortune has its part in human affairs,*
> *but conduct is really much more important.*
> JEANNE DETOURBEY

So when we feel unhappy about any situation that we find ourselves in, we can begin to look within ourselves for the solution by asking: "What am I doing to create this situation and in what way do I need to adjust in order for my life to improve?" There is a wonderful definition of insanity that says **"insanity is continuing to do the same things while expecting different results"**.

> *If you always do what you've always done,*
> *you'll always get what you've always got.*
> ANONYMOUS

8

TAKE RESPONSIBILITY

*If we continue to project
our problems outside of ourselves and
fail to recognise the inner power we actually have,
I believe we will support the very evils we are fighting.*
SHAKTI GAWAIN

Many people say that there are two main types of problem: those that are governed by our external circumstances and those that are created by our own internal disharmony. As you may already realise, these are connected since our external circumstances are a result of our consciousness.

Whenever we have a problem, it is very helpful if we can consider the possibility that it might have been created by our own consciousness or our own way of thinking. We must ask ourselves what patterns can I change within me to change the patterns that appear in my life? To change ourselves we need to become aware of the behavioural patterns that are causing the undesirable situations in our lives, this requires a considerable amount of self-observation.

Put your own house in order first.
PROVERB

This proverb is in great contrast to the unpleasant expression: "Look after number one" which implies that we should forget about others and only see to our own needs - this "what's in it for me?" attitude creates separation and isolation and is the path to loneliness, misery and suffering. Obviously, the above proverb isn't saying that we mustn't have care and consideration for others, it is implying that instead of judging, criticising, condemning or blaming others, we must look at what we need to work on within ourselves.

To be able to take care of others, we must first take care of ourselves.

Once we sort out our own emotional problems we will be in a much better position to help others with theirs. **We cannot be of service to others while we are weak and needy ourselves.** If a man is starving, he will find it difficult to feed others.

I once had a friend who was always upset about something or other and one day she said to me: "The problem with going on holiday is that you always have to take yourself with you!" It is quite clear that this person's problems were within her (and she knew it). Every situation was coloured by the negativity that she was carrying around. She was aware that even if she was put in the most beautiful place in the world she would still be miserable. Even if she were to be put in paradise she couldn't feel any joy from the experience because her internal disharmony would take away the value of the moment. It is clear that she would only become happier in life if she worked on developing her self-esteem to develop a positive self-image so that she could begin to love herself and feel happy about who she is.

There are some who say: "My problems are not internal, I have no lack of self-esteem, I am a good person, all my problems are due to external circumstances. If my wife was a bit more considerate with me and if I had more money I would be the happiest man in the world". This "victim" stance is never helpful because it implies that "my life will only improve if others change". It is true that just sometimes external circumstances "beyond our control" *might* be to blame, but we are nearly always responsible in some way, even if only indirectly, since our circumstances are a product of our consciousness. Every thought we think, every move we make and every decision we take goes towards determining our circumstances and these thoughts, actions and decisions depend on our own attitudes, beliefs, perceptions, hang-ups, behaviour and so on. It is in this way that we are responsible for the life we are leading and we must therefore learn to live with the awareness that we are completely responsible for our lives. **The only person who can make you happy in this life is you** - once you realise this, your control over your circumstances will increase enormously. We are not helpless victims at the mercy of friends, family and colleagues, but have an enormous influence in every situation. As soon as we begin to ask ourselves: "Am I responsible in any way for the situation that I am now in?" we begin to have control over doing something to improve our situation. This is the essence of self-empowerment. **You are free to think whatever you want to think in any situation, so why not choose positive thoughts of forgiveness, joy and empowerment?**

CONTROL YOUR OWN DESTINY

If we think that someone else needs to change for our life to improve then we are more likely to stay stuck. Try to keep in mind that **the only one you can change in this life is you**, unless someone requests your help because *they* want to change.

> *Realise that you cannot help a soul unless that soul really wants help and is ready to be helped.*
> EILEEN CADDY

We must try to accept people as they are, not as we want them to be. **Unconditional acceptance of another is the key to a deep friendship or relationship.**

If we try too hard to force others to live in our world,
because we think it is the real world,
we are doomed to disappointment.
WILLIAM GLASER, M.D.

Once you realise that you have the power to control and
determine your own destiny, your desire to control and
manipulate others will diminish. Strangely though, once you start
to live with this awareness and flow with life, others will
automatically and effortlessly go along *with you*, not against you,
without any manipulation being involved. It is also true that the
ability that others have to manipulate you will diminish once you
become aware of the incredible control that you have over your
own destiny.

As your desire to manipulate decreases,
your ability to influence increases.

**The less you need to be in control, the greater will be your
positive influence within your environment.** The "need" to
control often comes from an inner insecurity, lack of confidence
and feelings of self-doubt. As someone becomes more confident
and self-assured, their need to be in control by manipulating
others diminishes. A confident person is much better at seeing
disagreements from a point of view which is different to their
own.

Here is a crucially important question to ask yourself: do you
decide and control the events of your day or do the events of your
day control you? If someone is having problems at work or in
their relationship, it is the most natural thing in the world to say:
"If only he wouldn't do that" or "I wish she would be more
understanding". However, although it is totally natural to put the
blame onto something or someone else by complaining, this

attitude doesn't really get us anywhere because it comes from an underlying belief which says: "I am the victim of this unpleasant event or that horrible person - I am helpless." This attitude takes away our power and the feeling that we can do something about our situation.

To wait for someone else, or to expect someone else to make my life richer, or fuller, or more satisfying, puts me in a constant state of tension.
KATHLEEN TIERNEY ANDRUS

It is an interesting quirk of human nature that although people are more than willing to blame others for their "bad breaks" in life, most of us are more than willing to take personal credit for the "good breaks".

When a man blames others for his failures, it's a good idea to credit others with his successes.
HOWARD W. NEWTON

We can't have it both ways - either we take responsibility for both our successes and our failures, or we thank and blame the world for both. In fact "blame" is a very unhealthy state of mind which we would be better off avoiding altogether if at all possible.

Our ability to make things happen increases in direct proportion to our awareness that we have the ability to make things happen. If instead of feeling helpless, we realised the power we have to influence almost every situation, then the same internal conflict between, say, where we are now and where we want to be, will not cause a problem - on the contrary, it will provide the motivation that we need to spur us into action. We may be able to indirectly control or positively influence other people by setting a good example or giving friendly advice, but it is not helpful to try to control another's behaviour, beliefs, thoughts or attitudes directly. We have direct control only over our own behaviour, beliefs, thoughts and attitudes. But, as we change ourselves and adjust what is within us, everything outside will change automatically.

> *The world in which we live is not primarily determined by outward conditions and circumstances, but by the thoughts that habitually occupy the mind.*
> NORMAN VINCENT PEALE

As our awareness expands and we learn how our consciousness affects not only what is going on inside us but also what goes on outside us then we will realise the power that we have to influence our world for the better.

> *The world outside you is a reflection of the world inside you.*

LIFE IS YOUR MIRROR

> *A loving person lives in a loving world,*
> *A hostile person lives in a hostile world,*
> *Everyone you meet is your mirror.*
> KEN KEYES JR

The statement "life is your mirror" can be interpreted in a few ways. Since our life is a reflection of our consciousness, how others feel about us depends on what we give out, which, in turn is governed by how we feel about ourselves. The ideas that I want to convey within this section are encompassed within the following statements:

1)   The more you love yourself, the more others will love you.

2)   The more you love yourself, the easier you will find it to love others.

3)   The more you love others, the more others will love you.

Think carefully about each of these three statements before you read on. The last one is actually a statement of cause and effect which I will go into in more detail in the next chapter. For now I will deal with the first two statements.

The statement: *"The more you love yourself, the more others will love you"* is saying that all your relationships reflect your attitude and your feelings of self-worth; this can also be expressed as:

The more you see good in yourself,
the more others will see good in you.

How others see us is a reflection of how we feel about ourselves (as well as what is within them!) So, if for example you feel that nobody likes you, then this will be reflected in reality, because on a subtle level you transmit something which says: "I am not a very likeable person, so don't approach me". As I explained earlier, whenever we interact with someone, we are subconsciously conveying to them through our voice, body language and so on, how we feel about ourselves. You need to be your own friend for other people to want to be your friend. Another way of expressing this simple principle is:

You teach others how to treat you.
If you respect and trust yourself then others
will respect and trust you.

The second statement: *"The more you love yourself, the easier you will find it to love others"* can also be expressed as:

The more you see good in yourself
the more you will see good in others.

This principle is true, not only in relation to other people, but also towards life in general - **to feel good about life you have got to feel good about who you are.**

This principle works in a few ways:

1)   All your feelings for what is outside you are a reflection of the feelings within you, this depends to a large extent on all your previous conditioning.
2)   Your perceptions tend to mirror what is within you. You will not find much pleasure in the company of others if you don't like your own company.
3)   Your conditioning creates your actions, and the reactions of everyone and everything around you are a result of your actions. It is in this way that your circumstances reflect your level of consciousness.

These points are expressed in the following basic principle of life:

All our relationships are a reflection of
our relationship with ourselves.

The qualities, both good and bad, that you notice most clearly in another person are usually qualities that you possess yourself, so there is a fair amount of wisdom in that very simple expression: *"It takes one to know one".*

.....the part of the object's beauty
that stands out to each person, reflects back
qualities he or she already possesses.
JAMES REDFIELD/CAROL ADRIENNE

These last three quotations are slightly elaborate ways of expressing that most famous of sayings:

Beauty is in the eye of the beholder.
PROVERB

Think about that for a moment: if you see beauty in something, then that beauty is "within your eye". The fact that you can see beauty in something when someone else may not is a statement just as much about you as it is about the object of beauty.

All the loveliness of nature is but a reflection
of that which is within our souls.
HARI PRASAD SHASTRI

In fact, I believe that the perception of beauty is a measure of the interaction between the observer and the observed which involves a flow of energy between them, so it is a statement about connectedness rather than simply a flow of information into the eye of the observer.

To see the loveliness of nature, it is not enough to just have a beautiful essence, because if you are in turmoil you won't see the beauty. You must first find inner peace and then your perceptions of everything outside you will reflect this inner peace. I will return to this important point later.

It is interesting to consider that the Bible's statement that you should "love thy neighbour as thyself" doesn't take into account the fact that self-love may not be present, in which case neighbourly love would not account for very much! The more we develop our own inner beauty, the more we will be able to see beauty in those around us. Since this principle works both ways, if we notice someone with an irritating habit we must look carefully within ourselves to see if we too have that habit. Also, if we tend to criticise or judge someone for the way they behave, it could possibly be that we have that same negative characteristic lying dormant within us and for that reason it bothers us to see it in someone else.

So, next time you get irritated or angry with someone, have a good look at yourself. In the same way, if someone is very critical of you and always finds fault in what you do, you might see it as their own problem - they are probably seeing in you, characteristics that they don't like within themselves. However, if everyone has a low opinion of you, it might be very useful to have a good look at yourself to see what signals you are giving out or what it is that you are doing to create this impression.

Sometimes we may feel angry against an injustice perpetrated either against ourselves or against someone else. This is a totally natural, healthy emotion - what can sometimes be a problem is the way that the anger is expressed. It is important to be able to focus the energy of the anger constructively. It is also very important to realise that in a situation of *uncontrollable* anger, you are giving up your power to influence the situation for the better.

> *He who angers you, conquers you.*
> ELIZABETH KENNY

If a man feels angry with his partner he may consider it an unnecessary question to ask himself: "Is this anger arising from something within me that I need to work on, or is it really *all her fault*?" He may think that *it is obviously all her fault*. However, if his anger arises against, say, a machine which isn't working properly and doing exactly what he wants it to do, then it becomes fairly clear (especially to an outside observer), that his anger is his own problem, even though he may not realise it. In fact, whether our anger is against a machine or a person it is still *our* anger. **If you feel angry with someone, then you own that anger** - nobody gave it to you, and just as it was you who created that anger, it is you who must ultimately neutralise it.

The clearest illustration of how we deny the responsibility that we have for our own behaviour, thoughts and feelings is when they are against an inanimate object. A very clear example of this is illustrated by people who "blame" their credit cards for the fact that they are in debt, making statements such as: "If I didn't have that bloody credit card, then I wouldn't be in this mess now!" It is very clear that people with this attitude are not taking responsibility for their life.

You own, not only your anger, but *every* other feeling that you may have - you own your depression, your misery, your inner turmoil, your inner peace and your happiness.

> *If other people are annoying you,*
> *it's not they who are being annoying,*
> *it's you who is being annoyed.*
> MONICA DICKENS

YOU CAN CHANGE

Did you ever wonder how it would feel
to be a grub and then turn into a winged creature?
It helps us to endure the depressing passage if we can remember
that we're being prepared for a new stage of our lives, one in
which, perhaps, we will leave our old selves
as far behind as the dragonfly leaves the larva.
KAREN CASEY / MARTHA VANCEBURG

Do you ever feel like the ugly duckling who is on the point of
becoming a beautiful swan, or a caterpillar on its way to
becoming a butterfly? It is important to realise that you are, in
essence, already beautiful, even if you don't realise it yet. For
many, the most important step in self-development comes from
acknowledging one's own inner beauty.

What is a weed?
A plant whose virtues have not been discovered.
RALPH WALDO EMERSON

When someone feels self-dissatisfaction and wants to change,
they are usually focusing on fairly superficial characteristics and
not looking at who they really are.

Once you can acknowledge your own inner beauty,
then the butterfly will be ready to emerge.

There is a very common expression which states that "a leopard
never changes his spots". This is usually used when someone
wants to express that a person will never change, but whether it is
true or not depends on whether we are talking about the person's
character or *behaviour*.   When it refers to behaviour it is

definitely not valid, as it is very possible for someone to change their behaviour *if they want to change*. But the expression is more often used to refer to someone's character, and in this case it is *almost* true to say that it is valid. However, it does depend on what aspect of character we are referring to, and, most importantly, it depends on how strongly they themselves want to change. If someone is very eccentric, very serious, or very sensitive, these are characteristics that are fairly unchangeable, (although they are not impossible to change if someone is sufficiently motivated and really works on themselves). However, a leopard can "change his spots" if we are referring to conditioned characteristics - which are really more like habits - such as shyness. Someone can certainly become more sociable, confident, friendly and outgoing as an act of will if they so wish, and although initially their new *behaviour* may be a little forced, after a short while it will become their "natural state", and so their "character" will slowly change.

Bill and Pat are partners who often have little disagreements. The following argument illustrates a confusion that some have between changing character and behaviour.

Bill: Oh no, you've left the milk out of the fridge again.
Pat: Don't pick on me for such trivia.
Bill: But you know it annoys me, I don't like using milk that's warm or sour, can you please remember to put it back in future?
Pat: Listen, you shouldn't expect me to change, that's just the way I am, if you don't like it hard luck.
Bill: I don't expect you to change, I am only telling you not to leave the milk out of the fridge!
Pat: Well that sounds to me like you *are* expecting me to change. I think *you* should change, don't get so irritated by trivia, and try to get used to the way I am, I am not going to change and that's that.

In this argument, Pat is confusing character and behaviour. She has heard that in a relationship you have got to accept people as they are and is misinterpreting this as not complaining about someone's behaviour. Leaving milk out of the fridge is nothing to do with character and it is very easy to change a habit like this. However, Bill's problem of getting irritated is more closely related to character than behaviour and is much more difficult to change. But, having said that, Bill could, if he was sufficiently self-motivated, become more accepting and less judgemental of his partner's habits, and he would then not get so irritated with her.

So, if someone has the habit of swearing when they speak, always leaving the top off the toothpaste tube, walking in the house with muddy shoes or leaving the milk out of the fridge, then it is an invalid excuse for them to say: "Well, that's just the way I am".

It is very important to be aware that there are many so-called characteristics that we may have that are simply habits that we have picked up during the course of our lives. Although a person's way of thinking may often be considered to be an innate characteristic, it may in fact be a mental habit. The clearest example of this is the worry habit. Someone may say "I am a worrier" as if it is a characteristic that they have like a big nose or brown eyes, but this isn't the case, since worry is not a property of character, it is just a mental habit that has been picked up that can be changed like any other habit.

There is such a thing as positive worry which is focusing on a problem with the intention of finding a solution, but this is different to what most people do when they worry. They simply focus on the problem, thinking about how unfortunate they are, what an impossible situation they are in and how much worse things are going to get. In its most common and destructive form the imagination sets up an unpleasant mental state by thinking about future moments and picturing things going wrong.

> *To have a crisis, and act upon it, is one thing;*
> *to dwell in perpetual crisis is another.*
> BARBARA GRIZZUTI HARRISON

Dwelling in crisis doesn't get us anywhere. This type of worry is not an innate characteristic and there is no evolutionary value for this unfortunate psychological condition which creates dissatisfaction, dampens the quality of life and hampers self-development because of the fear of risk.

So, in conclusion, it is very possible to change your behaviour and it is even possible, if you are determined enough, to change certain habitual characteristics that you may have always considered are fixed personal traits. But be careful that the motivation doesn't come from self-hatred, guilt or any other self-sabotaging state, since this is nearly always counter-productive. Try to be motivated more by how you would like to be rather than by how you don't want to be.

THE POWER OF ATTENTION

> *Where attention goes, energy flows.*
> JAMES REDFIELD/CAROL ADRIENNE

When we put our attention on something, we are focusing the energy of our consciousness upon it. If we always put our attention on what we don't have or what we don't like, we will probably spend a lot of time and energy grumbling and complaining about life. Where does this energy go? Well, a good proportion of it goes towards producing disharmony within us that can lead to ill health, or at the very least, tiredness, lethargy or exhaustion, and the rest of it goes on enhancing the very thing that we are complaining about.

The quality of one's life depends on the quality of attention. Whatever you pay attention to will grow more important in your life.
DEEPAK CHOPRA

If someone's attention is always on what they don't want in life, then their attention, and hence their energy, is not available, not only to pursue, but even to discover, that which they do want. For this reason it is important to put our attention on what we want in life - on our goals and dreams rather than on our dreads and fears.

The quality of attention that we give to others is also of vital importance. When we "pay" attention to someone, they change in some way from "the payment", because we are feeding them with a kind of emotional energy - we are literally "paying" attention. If we pay attention to someone's "unworthy" characteristic then this negative aspect of their character will grow. If we pay attention to someone's stinginess then they will become more stingy. If we pay attention to someone's laziness then they will become more lazy. If we pay attention to someone's weakness then they will become weaker. If we pay attention to someone's greediness then they will become more greedy. Conversely, the same will happen if we pay attention to someone's positive qualities.

If we pay attention to someone's generosity, kindness and strength, then they will become more generous, kind and strong.

This is especially true of our own qualities and how we see ourselves. The less time we spend putting attention on our own faults, the easier it will be to see the good qualities that we have, and in this way we will develop in a healthy way. Most of us seem to notice the bad in ourselves, others, events and situations of life more than we notice the good. Everyone has both desirable and undesirable characteristics, but most people tend to focus on, and criticise, the undesirable ones and ignore the good qualities. If you meet someone with nine wonderful qualities and one bad one, do you notice and focus on the one negative aspect of their character, or on all the good qualities?

Since the qualities which we pay attention to in someone tend to grow, the best thing that we can do if someone has a negative characteristic that we don't like, is just ignore it, although this is easier said than done if someone close to us has an irritating habit or engages in unpleasant behaviour. However, our own self-esteem will rise if we can practice ignoring or overlooking the negative characteristics in others and learn to praise and compliment the positive.

> *Anyone can blame;*
> *it takes a specialist to praise.*
> KONSTANTIN STANISLAVSKI

Many people find it difficult to praise others because they feel that they are somehow putting themselves down if they speak highly of another. However, in reality, the reverse is true - the more confident and secure a person is, the easier they find it to praise others, pay compliments, make people feel good and show appreciation for everything that they receive from those around them. If we are over-critical and we really try, it is possible to find fault with anyone or anything.

Faults can be found even in saints and angels,
if they are seen through a judgemental eye.

If someone spends the day doing housework and does twenty things but misses one, then *obviously* when their partner comes home they will notice the one thing that hasn't been done, instead of appreciating all the things that have. I say "obviously" because although this isn't a very nice response, it is natural to a certain extent. By analogy, if you have twenty light bulbs in front of you and one of them is faulty and keeps flashing on and off, then you will notice the faulty one before the others. If, as you read this book, you find one statement that you disagree with out of a hundred that you agree with, then when commenting upon the book to someone else you are more likely to focus on the statement that you disagreed with rather than on all those that you agreed with.

Be fair in thy judgement,
and guarded in thy speech.
BAHA'I FAITH

It is far easier to notice the negative in something and the faults in someone, but we will develop a healthier outlook if we practice focusing on the good, positive qualities of everyone and everything in our lives. These principles apply not only to our interactions with adults but also when we are with children, even more so, in fact. Many people believe that a child can be spoiled if they are given too much attention, however, this is definitely not the case.

Loving attention is the most valuable
gift that you could give a child.

26

It is not at all a bad thing to give a child lots of attention, the mistake that many parents make is to give them the attention only when they are behaving badly - thus rewarding their bad behaviour. This is impossible to avoid sometimes but it should be minimised wherever possible. I witnessed an example recently in a shop, which illustrates this point exactly - a child was trying to get his fathers attention saying, "Daddy, Daddy", while tugging on his trouser leg - he got no response. He continued for another minute or so - still with no response. The child then threw down his toy and yelled *"DADDY"* in a very loud, frustrated voice - his father then turned to him and said "yes, what do you want?" Sadly, he didn't get the reward of his father's attention while he was behaving well, but he received the "reward" when he became aggressive, so he will learn that aggression receives reward.

In all our interactions with children or with adults we should try to respond well to positive behaviour and overlook or minimise our response towards the negative. The times to give a child our full, undivided attention are when they are behaving well, ensuring that the attention contains a lot of love and useful information. If attention is given at this time and in this way then it is impossible to say "that child gets too much attention."

The best way to deal with a child who you think has a negative characteristic, is to ignore it and to point out and reward the child whenever they show the opposite, positive characteristic. For example, if a child has a weight problem due to eating too much, don't draw attention to their gluttony whenever they are having dinner, but instead congratulate them on how well they are doing when they go a certain time without eating. Conversely, if a child never seems to want to eat anything, try to avoid giving them the self-image of being "a child who doesn't like eating", since, once this happens, a problem can be created when there previously wasn't one. We can apply similar rules to the way that we treat ourselves too, so that we reward ourselves for our achievements rather than punish ourselves for our failings.

James was a little boy who sometimes appeared a bit lazy and because his father believed in the importance of working hard to get on in life, he kept pointing out how lazy James was, making statements such as: "James you shouldn't be such a lazy boy, go and tidy your room" and "James, you'll never get anywhere in life if you don't work hard". Also, in the company of others he would make comments such as: "James hates studying or reading, he just wants to sit and watch T.V. all day." The effect of this was to give James a self-image of being a lazy person and he then inevitably lived up to this image by actually becoming a lazy person. What James's father could have done is overlook the laziness whenever he noticed it, but compliment him and give him plenty of attention whenever he showed an effort.

LEARN FROM EVERY EXPERIENCE

I do not reach to heights I cannot yet attain,
I reach only where I am and climb with life;
It is the only teacher I yearn for
- the greatest teacher of all -
a thousand million years old,
yet forever as young as each day.
ANDREA PHOTIOU

Suppose that you have two paths in front of you. One path provides you with pleasures for the senses - delicious cakes and sweets, T.V. and video entertainments and a whole variety of sensual pleasures. The other path contains food for the soul -

meditation and relaxation, exercise, healthy foods, wise people, hard experiences and so on. The first path is enjoyable but at the end of the journey you feel a bit sick. The second path is less stimulating and exciting to the senses than the first but at the end of the journey you feel a wonderful sense of achievement. Which path would you choose?

When presented with both choices it is very natural to choose the first. We find it so difficult to do what is best for the soul not the senses. It is food for the spirit that gives rise to the most wonderful feelings even though the sensory stimulation appears so much more attractive.

> *The wise man chooses the path of joy;*
> *the fool takes the path of pleasure.*
> KATHA UPANISHAD 2

Sometimes it is hard to see the reason for a bad experience, when this is the case, we could try to look at the situation as if we were an external observer viewing the event from outside. In this way we will see things in a different light and learn more from the experience than if we were wrapped up in "our problem", just wishing it wasn't happening.

> *Experience is not what happens to you;*
> *it is what you do with what happens to you.*
> ALDOUS HUXLEY

Every experience that we have, whether good or bad, can teach us something, so we will develop faster if we can get into the habit of asking ourselves the question: **"What can I learn from this?"** Sometimes we can't immediately see it, especially if it is a very unpleasant situation, but it is up to us to try to discover the reason behind each event that occurs in our lives. Every time we come up against an obstacle, we have the choice to see it either as a problem that we are the victim of, or as a challenge that life is giving us to help our growth.

It is possible to go through life totally over-looking the things that could give us so much joy and happiness if we could only realise it. Every situation that confronts us can teach us something if we are open to the lessons that life is offering us.

> *Everyone and everything around you*
> *is your teacher.*
> *KEN KEYES JR*

The hard things that happen in life often give us the best lessons that we can have and it helps enormously in trying to come to terms with the unchangeable aspects of life to believe that **everything happens for a reason.**

> *Events that seem "accidental" are drawn in by people to*
> *heal themselves of their old beliefs and patterns.*
> *SHAKTI GAWAIN*

Everyone that we meet comes into our lives to teach us something, and we can learn from every interaction with every human being. But we need to know how to openly listen and take in the messages that life is giving us. If we can see the value in every situation then we will progress much faster along our path. **Life is a succession of experiences for our growth and development.**

> *Just accept life as it is and go with the flow,*
> *every lesson that you live tells you what you need to know.*

We always receive our lessons at the right time, when we are ready to receive them, someone may tell us something that might be very useful for us but we won't hear it unless we are ready to hear it. The same applies as we read a book or talk to someone - **we are only able to notice what we are ready to notice.** And when we are ready, we learn from the simplest things.

> *Anything you say to a wise man*
> *will make him wiser.*
> PROVERBS 9, 9

There are many people whose aim in life is to try and get to a position where there will be no obstacles, challenges or hardships. These people dream about a wonderful time in the future when it will no longer be necessary to work and they can just sit on the beach all day sipping cocktails. This is a very idyllic image, but to live like this wouldn't be healthy for anyone's development. Maybe the occasional day would be wonderful, but in general, we develop much more healthily due to life's challenges and difficulties. So, if our aim is to develop and progress in life, then we shouldn't really want everything to be easy and idyllic.

> *One often learns more from ten days of agony*
> *than from ten years of contentment.*
> MERLE SHAIN

When someone is in a difficult relationship there is always a tendency to want to split up, run away - do anything but confront the difficult situation. However, if we can live with the awareness that we chose this person to learn a special lesson, and if we separate before learning the lesson then history will undoubtedly repeat itself until we learn what we need to learn. Many people go from a bad relationship into a new and wonderful relationship only to find that within a short time similar conflicts start coming up again. These "patterns" don't just come up by coincidence, we attract them into our lives to learn what we need to learn according to our level of consciousness. And history will continue to repeat itself until we learn the lesson that life is trying to teach us from that situation.

Many religions express the idea in some way that suffering brings us closer to God, increases our appreciation for life and teaches us the exact lessons that we need for our growth.

Tests are benefits from God,
for which we should thank him.
Grief and sorrow do not come to us by chance,
they are sent to us for our own perfecting.
The more a man suffers, the greater is
the harvest of spiritual values shown forth by him.
BAHA'I FAITH

It is not only the hard knocks that life gives us that we can learn and develop from, it is also the hard decisions that we have to take. The things that we find most difficult to do often provide the best lessons for us.

It is not our smooth passages that reveal new understandings,
but the strenuous, uphill battles that benefit us with
the knowledge we need to grow.
KAREN CASEY / MARTHA VANCEBURG

Be Good
To Others

BE GOOD TO OTHERS

If one could be made to understand that caring
only for oneself is bondage, while
feeding others is freedom,
then life would be easy for all.
SHANTANAND SARASWATI.

Every religion has expressed in one form or another that if we live our lives selfishly and cause problems and suffering everywhere we go, then we will inevitably bring misery and pain upon ourselves. Here are three quotations from Hinduism, Buddhism and Christianity that express this view, each in their own way:

If a man speaks or acts with an evil thought,
pain follows him.
HINDU PROVERB

Cease to do evil and purify your heart.
THE BUDDHA

Wicked people bring about
their own downfall by their evil deeds,
but good people are protected by their integrity.
PROVERBS 14, 32

The last of these draws our attention to the important fact that goodness needs integrity to flourish. The basis of our happiness is governed, not so much by what is provided to us from outside, but more on our thoughts, words, beliefs and deeds - if we keep these healthy, we will be happy and successful.

The fruits that we yield from life are the results of our own actions, this in turn depends on our level of awareness. The position that we are in now is a result of our past behaviour and, in the same way, **our behaviour at this moment is creating our future.**

*The quality of your life will be determined by
the quality of your behaviour.*
THE BUDDHA

We must treat others fairly and gently if that's how we want to be treated.

*Give kind words, be helpful and be consistent
between word and deed.*
THE BUDDHA

THE LAW OF CAUSE AND EFFECT

*Those who act kindly in this world
will have kindness.*
QUR'AN 39.10

It is one of the most fundamental of all scientific assumptions that every effect has a cause, and that nothing happens without something to cause it to happen. This applies to every aspect of life from the laws of physics to what happens whenever we talk to another person or smile at someone. Two thousand years ago Jesus expressed the law of cause and effect in the following simple way:

Whatsoever a man soweth that shall he also reap.
JESUS CHRIST

This law of cause and effect is one of the most fundamental principles of both science and religion, and every religion expresses it in one form or another.

Actions are like invisible seeds planted in the unborn.
If the seed is good the fruit will be good,
if the seed is bad the fruit will be bad.
Every action of body, speech and mind
is subject to this natural law.
THE BUDDHA

This is so obvious and yet so many live their lives sowing bad seeds and then feel anger and resentment when they reap a bad harvest. They go through life never smiling at anyone *because* nobody ever smiles at them, and they may be nasty to people because they think that people are nasty to them.

Don't expect to receive friendship, love and joy,
if you are giving out hostility, anger and misery.

Jesus also expressed this universal law as:

Whatsoever a man sends out in word or deed
will return to him.
JESUS CHRIST

Once we realise that in life we reap what we sow, then it is ridiculous and self-detrimental to be nasty, hateful or treat people with disrespect. **The effects that we get are created by the causes that we initiate.**

The game of life is a game of boomerangs.
Our thoughts, deeds, and words return to us sooner or later,
with astounding accuracy.
FLORENCE SCOVEL SHINN

In the East this process of action and reaction is called karma and in Eastern religions it is said that we *always* pay the consequences for our behaviour if we act badly - sooner or later it will catch up with us.

No person in the world ever attempted to wrong
another without being injured in return
- some way, somehow, sometime.
WILLIAM GEORGE JORDAN

No thought or action is without results. Sometimes, it may appear that a criminal never receives an appropriate punishment for his crimes, however, Eastern religions teach that if a man doesn't suffer the consequences of his evil deeds in this life-time, then he will in the next.

At the moment of death.....
.....there arises before man's mind,
the vision of his life to come,
a vision regulated by his impressions of his past deeds.....
HINDUISM - SRIMAD BHAGAVATAM 11.15

If you relate the law of cause and effect to your everyday interactions with people, it makes very clear that very well-known saying:

Do as you would be done by.
RELIGIOUS PROVERB.

It is always true to say that **what you give out you get back.**
This is not only a spiritual or behavioural principle - it is also
expressed in physics by the following very important physical
law discovered by Sir Isaac Newton in the seventeenth century:

Every action has an equal and opposite reaction.
SIR ISAAC NEWTON

This is called Newton's third law and is just another expression of
the law of cause and effect. What it means, literally, is that if a
force is exerted on an object then that object will exert an equal
force in return. Relating Newton's third law to your everyday
life, if the action is to do good the reaction will be to receive
good.

The more good you do to others,
the more good others will do to you.

This is true in every aspect of your life. Human beings are
basically very adaptable and responsive to incoming messages
and we tend to reflect upon each other - laughter breeds laughter,
honesty breeds honesty, love breeds love, and so on.

As contagion of sickness makes sickness,
contagion of trust can make trust.
MARIANNE MOORE

Unfortunately, it must also be true that when you have negative
thoughts or feelings of aggression, hate or rivalry, then that
negativity bounces back on you - anger breeds anger,
aggressiveness breeds aggressiveness, hate breeds hate and so on.

Do not speak harshly to anybody,
for they will answer you in the same way.
Angry speech breeds trouble;
you shall receive blows for blows.
THE DHAMMAPADA 133

If someone lives their lives only for themselves, accumulating wealth and focusing all their efforts on materialistic success, not caring about who they tread on or exploit, they will never have enough to find the fulfilment and inner joy that they so desperately and blindly seek.

Never in the world is hatred conquered by hatred;
hatred is conquered by love.
THE DHAMMAPADA 223.5

The law of cause and effect is true not only of the big things we do but of every single move we make. **If you genuinely do something nice for another person you create in them the desire to do something nice for you.** But it is better if the nice act isn't only done with the intention of receiving a reward in return but simply because we want to give another person pleasure.

Do not be content with showing friendship in words alone,
let your heart burn with loving kindness
for all who may cross your path.
BAHA'I FAITH

If you spend your time trying to improve the lives of everyone that you interact with, what do you think will be the effect on you?

Be generous and you will be prosperous.
Help others and you will be helped.
PROVERBS 11, 25

The usual view of a cancer cell is one of a fast growing cell which is out of control. This has much in common with a person living totally selfishly and, on one level, it can be said to be functioning very successfully from its own selfish viewpoint. It only cares about itself and not the good of the whole - it takes in all the goodness that it can from the tissue fluid that it is bathed in without consideration for the cells around it - its considerations are simply to satisfy its own gluttony and reproductive needs, spreading more of its own kind throughout the organism. In this way it thrives for a short while, but living like this is ultimately self-destructive, since although it grows quickly it inevitably kills the life that supports it. A man who lives *just* for himself is very much like a cancer cell, and ultimately destroys himself in much the same way.

When we harm others, we harm ourselves.
When we heal others, we heal ourselves.

Try to hold good feelings of love, kindness and appreciation within you, not only towards people but also towards life itself. It is easier to fear life than to trust life, but life will respond according to how you feel about it just as a person will. **If you give out good feelings towards life and have respect towards it, then that's what you will get back.** Smile at life, and life will smile at you.

Do all the good you can,
by all the means you can,
in all the ways you can,
in all the places you can,
at all the times you can,
to all the people you can,
as long as ever you can.
JOHN WESLEY

It is very important to realise that in giving comfort to others you will feel comforted yourself - in giving love you will receive it - or in the words of one of the greatest song-writing duos of all time:

And in the end
the love you take,
is equal to
the love you make.
LENNON/MCCARTNEY

GIVING AND RECEIVING

You find true joy and happiness in life when you
give and give and go on giving
and never count the cost.
EILEEN CADDY

Nature designed there to be a perfect balance between giving and receiving. Most of the great religions of the world point out that when we reach the end of our lives **the truest measure of how much we will have achieved is not in how much we have managed to accumulate but in how much we have given**

away. If we are to have any regrets when we reach the end of the road in this life, it is not very likely to be "If only I spent more time at the office", it is more likely to be "If only I gave my loved ones more time and expressed more love".

If you take much more than you ever give,
you end up with less than you started with.
ANDREA PHOTIOU

When Jesus talked about giving he certainly wasn't only referring to material giving, there are many ways to give which don't involve money such as a favour, a word of advice or a teaching, love or emotional support, our time, a compliment, words of encouragement, our full attention for a few moments or simply a smile. To give a word of advice can often be far more valuable than anything material. To teach someone something useful is a much more permanent and far-reaching gift than anything material that you could give.

Give a man a fish and he'll eat for a day,
teach a man to fish and he'll eat for a life-time.
PROVERB

The best thing that we can do to accelerate our own spiritual development is to give help to someone else with a genuine love and concern. In many cases the greatest way that we can help someone is by assisting them to increase their level of awareness.

Every truth we see is one to give to the world,
not to keep to ourselves alone.
ELIZABETH CADY STANTON

If what we receive is true wisdom, we will *know* when it is right to share our insights. **In receiving light, love or wisdom we**

tend to act as mirrors re-transmitting the goodness that we receive.

There are two ways of spreading light:
to be the candle or the mirror that reflects it.
EDITH WHARTON

The value of giving someone advice from the heart, when it is asked for, is immense, and when we do this we may be surprised to hear ourselves saying things that we didn't even realise we knew - this is wisdom coming from within. However, to try to give helpful advice when it is not requested can do more harm than good since it tends to set up a distance between people. This is especially true when the advice is related to religious dogma rather than wisdom from the heart. Offering the ideas of a religious doctrine in order to save others from "eternal sin" is probably one of the clearest examples possible of advice that can often do more harm than good.

It is usually very difficult to be generous towards a miserly person. However, although it may be difficult to be charitable or generous towards someone who appears not to deserve it and who may seem very stingy and closed, it is the best way to make them realise the error of their ways.

One of the highest forms of charity
is unselfish giving to a person who appears
unworthy of the gift.

Some people may give money or a gift, not because they want something back of similar value in return, but because they want appreciation or to be seen as a generous person. This is not a bad thing but it is not as spiritual as unconditional giving - this is where the ego isn't involved in the process of giving. If we are able to give truly from the heart the rewards in the long run are far, far greater than if we give for ego building intentions.

*Perhaps the closest we can
come to a pure gift is an anonymous one......
Such a gift, which can never be acknowledged or returned
by those it comforts, can heal our spirits when
they are wearied by too much ego.*
KAREN CASEY / MARTHA VANCEBURG

It is also very important to consider the fact that if we can't bring ourselves to give, unless we are going to be acknowledged or thanked, then maybe we are not truly giving from the heart, since this shows that our giving is really done with the intention of getting something back in return. **The more we give without expecting a reward, the greater will be our reward.**

*When we give from a place of love,
rather than from a place of expectation,
more usually comes back to us than
we could ever have imagined.*
SUSAN JEFFERS

Stingy people may not receive much because they are too frightened to give - they cling on to their money and stop the natural universal process of flow which occurs when we are able to relax our attitude to money and realise that it will come as easily as it goes.

*Give without being paid,
and you will receive without paying.*
MATTHEW 10, 8

Although a person who gives less *might*, as a result, have a greater accumulation of wealth it certainly won't lead to the satisfaction and contentment that they might expect it to, since the quality of every human interaction will be less open and giving. It is obvious that a stingy person won't receive the same rewards in life as a generous person, this is a natural consequence of the law of cause and effect. **When we hold back from giving to others, others hold back from giving to us.**

> *Give and it will be given to you,*
> *for the measure you give will be*
> *the measure you get back.*
> *LUKE 6, 38*

Although this expression of the law of cause and effect may often be interpreted as referring to financial income and material wealth, it obviously applies to giving at all levels. It is often the spiritual things in life such as love and friendship that bring the richest feelings of "wealth".

> *Oh shrewd businessman, do only profitable business:*
> *deal only in that commodity which shall*
> *accompany you after death.*
> *SIKHISM - ADI GRANTH, SRI RAGA*

FINDING TRUE SECURITY

It is an interesting observation to notice that within our society it is very difficult to meet someone who thinks that they have enough money. This applies to every income bracket - no one ever earns as much as they would like. Also many people think that they will have financial "security" once they are earning a certain amount. This is obviously an illusion, just as it is an illusion to think that one day I will be happy when I meet the perfect partner, have a nice sports car, have my own house, or whatever. I will discuss this further in the next chapter.

I have often wondered "what is it that makes some people so generous and others so miserly?" Obviously, the answer has very little to do with material wealth; it has more to do with our attitudes towards life and money. It is true that if we are financially poor then it is more difficult for most of us to be generous because the ego tends to generate thoughts such as "will I have enough left for myself?" If we have plenty of money in the bank it is easier to give because we can then feel that "there's always more where that came from". But some people have much that they could give, but instead cling onto everything they have. What causes this holding back? Why does it sometimes feel so difficult to give? What determines how much we are able to give in life?

The main factor that determines our generosity more than our wealth, is related to how secure we feel about our ability to replenish what we have given. **We find it difficult to give if we fear that what we have given out won't be replenished. True security means trusting in life**

We can never find true security in the things outside of us; it comes from believing that the universe, life or people are on our side.

Material giving becomes easier not so much when we have plenty of money in the bank such that we won't even notice the difference, but more when we can develop the feeling that life is on our side and replenishment will automatically occur. This means that true generosity, whether financial or otherwise, depends more on a person's inner feeling of security than on how much they have to give.

Security is not a measure of how much life gives us;
it is more a measure of how much trust we
have in life to provide for our needs.

Just as happiness comes from within, so too does security. It is the thought "When I have .... then I will be happy", that keeps us unhappy. Similarly, it is the thought "When I have .... then I will feel secure", that keeps us feeling insecure. As soon as we can develop a sincere trust in life, then we will instantly become more secure and therefore find it much easier to be generous.

Although it may be the case that true generosity is giving our last penny and not worrying about ourselves, I think that this type of totally unselfish giving is not easily achievable for the average person, and we mustn't berate ourselves if we find it difficult to give up our last penny to feed a stranger. This type of giving is what is characteristic of the saintly people of this world such as Mother Teresa and many other unsung heroes who devote their time to helping others. Although this type of giving is difficult to attain, it is what we could all be aspiring to since the greatest pleasure that we can experience is to know that we are genuinely helping the life of another.

To take away something from yourself to give to another,
that is humane and gentle and never takes away
as much comfort as it brings again.
 THOMAS MORE

In the same way as the ease with which we give money depends on our feelings of financial security, the ease with which we give love depends on our emotional security. For someone to be loving they need to feel loved, or at least that they are worthy of being loved. It's obvious really that the more love you have inside, the more love you will have to give. **The richness of our lives depends on the quality of the love that we both give and receive.**

When we learn how to truly give,
we will know how to truly live.

Before leaving this section I would just like to mention an *apparent* contradiction to the law of cause and effect that may sometimes be experienced. There are some people who are very generous, give in many ways, and yet don't seem to receive much in return. Why should this be? This doesn't seem to be consistent with the law of cause and effect.

The answer lies in the fact that they may not feel that they are worthy of receiving, which causes an imbalance in the natural flow of energy and blocks the channel to freely receive, making life less rich. It is possible for someone to do this on a totally subconscious level. I have met people who are so generous, but because of their subconscious programming which says "I am not worthy enough to receive anything really good", they stop good fortune from coming into their lives. They may wonder why they never have enough money or good fortune, not realising it is because they are subconsciously blocking the flow.

Some are kept in poverty by saying: "I want to be rich but I don't believe that I ever will be", while others are kept in poverty by saying: "Money isn't important to me, I don't want to be rich".

There is a famous proverb that is often misquoted as: "money is the root of all evil", the correct quotation is actually:

The love of money is the root of all evil.
1 TIMOTHY 6,10

Once we realise that we may be creating blocks by either our conscious attitudes and beliefs, or our subconscious programming, we can begin to remove these barriers and allow the natural flow of money both away from and towards us. Those who have negative attitudes towards money, may say that this is encouraging greed and attachment, but often the reverse might be true - as the blocks are removed money becomes less of an issue and so greed and attachment simply disappear.

Money is simply a convenient representation of goods and services and so to block the flow of money is to block the flow of what we can both give to the world and what we can receive from it. It is very important to realise that **a person can only receive what they believe they are worthy of receiving.**

Lack of money reflects the
subconscious blocks within us.

ACCEPT OTHERS AS THEY ARE

To know how to respect the essence
of others though they may be blind to it
themselves, recognising the need to learn from and
touch each other, builds strong foundations
in this earthly life. In this way the
seeds of love begin to germinate.
ANDREA PHOTIOU

To try to change others sets up barriers which only result in ill-feeling and animosity between people. You know that you are happiest when you are in the company of a person who makes you feel good about yourself. If you turn this around then it is obvious that someone else will prefer to be in your company if you make them feel good about themselves. Every day holds at least some opportunity to help make another person feel good, and if you live your life trying to make others feel good then you will feel happier about who you are. **If you live your life trying to raise the self-esteem of others then your own self-esteem will rise.**

The only reward of virtue is virtue;
the only way to have a friend is to be one.
RALPH WALDO EMERSON

A question that is very important to consider is "should we avoid negative people?" Many would say that we should avoid negative people because they sap our life-force, absorb our energy, deflate our confidence, stop us having good feelings towards events or people and take away our feelings of positivity and trust in life. However, if the negative people in our lives are just casual acquaintances it may be easy to avoid them, but what if members of our family or our partner is only able to see the bad side of life, what should we do then? Well, I think that if this is the case we need to look at their negativity as a challenge for our own growth and development by trying to:

1)   Be immune to their negativity so that their "negative states" are not passed on to us - *don't be negative about their negativity!*

2)	Help to improve their view of life, not by trying to change them but by simply showing a better way to live and look at life.

Ultimately they will not change unless *they* want to change their outlook on life and become more positive. We can't change them only because *we* want them to change, so we mustn't expect to. Separation from the negative person could be considered if the person's negativity is of such a degree that they stop us from developing, and if they distrust life so much that we feel they don't allow us to have trust in life ourselves.

The situation with negative friends is very different since we probably don't have the same type of commitment towards casual friends and acquaintances as we do towards our partner. If they are always expressing how horrible the world is then we could try one of two courses of action:

1)	Stop being in their company. Try to make friends with people who are going to make us see life in a more optimistic way.

2)	Look at their negativity or their bad moods as "an external event" which doesn't need to pull us down or rub off on us. In a similar way to how the weather outside can be seen in a positive way, so too can the "gloomy weather" in the home or at work be looked at with a positive attitude.

Another reason that we may want to avoid certain people is if they bring out unpleasant aspects of our character? You may only want to be with the people who bring out the best in you and keep away from those who might bring out the worst, but is this a wise way to live? I think not. We develop from the challenges of life, so we can have a certain appreciation for those people in our lives who give us the need to work on ourselves. If someone makes us angry, irritated, judgemental, or resentful, we may have a tendency to want to avoid them. However, these people can help us to develop if we can internally thank them for helping us to draw our attention to the things that we need to work on within ourselves.

I have learnt silence from the talkative;
tolerance from the intolerant;
and kindness from the unkind.
I should not be ungrateful to those teachers.
KAHLIL GIBRAN

I once met a Buddhist monk who described how he was able to attain a profound sense of inner peace, tranquillity and love for all humanity while he was living as a hermit, meditating on his own, but as soon as he moved back into society and had to start interacting with other people, irritations and petty annoyances would immediately arise. We need to develop the good within us and learn to develop self-respect, inner peace, love, and so on, but if we can only do this while we are surrounded by angels then we may be deluding ourselves.

We can learn a considerable amount by observing negative traits in another person. Maybe, to eliminate our own negativity, we need to make use of the lessons we can learn from watching the negativity in others.

It takes a thorn to remove a thorn.
HINDU PROVERB

We all have the capacity for great selfishness or for great love and compassion, but we need to patiently look at those aspects of our character that we may not be that pleased with - the "difficult" people in our lives can sometimes help us with these.

(I put the word difficult in speech marks because the difficulty is not always in them, it may often be in our perception of them).

We all know, that people are the same wherever you go, there is good and bad in everyone.
PAUL MCCARTNEY AND STEVIE WONDER.
(EBONY AND IVORY)

We can learn an important lesson in avoiding conflict if we can avoid *reacting* to situations, but instead learn to *respond* with awareness. We all react to a certain extent, not only in response to the present situation, but also according to our conditioning. We will learn a great lesson in avoiding conflict if we are able to respond to any situation as it is rather than react in a way which is a result of previous negative experiences. We will become more successful if we can learn to respond in such a way that we neither trivialise what is important nor exaggerate what is unimportant, in other words to weigh up each situation on its own merits.

Decency of mind means to think appropriate thoughts, to respond properly to events and people, neither exaggerating nor trivialising their importance.
KAREN CASEY / MARTHA VANCEBURG

As I said earlier, positivity breeds positivity and negativity breeds negativity, however, in spite of the fact that this action/reaction response is fairly natural, there is a certain hypocrisy in judging the judgemental, getting angry with the irritable, being nasty to the unkind, and so on.

Do not judge if you do not want to be judged; do not condemn if you do not want to be condemned.
JESUS CHRIST

DON'T JUDGE - LOVE.

If you judge people you have no time to love them.
MOTHER TERESA

The quality of attention that we give in our social interactions depends on how judgemental or non-judgemental we are. Although, for most of us, it is fairly unrealistic to totally avoid any kind of judgement, it is nevertheless well worthwhile if we can work towards achieving this goal, since the less critical and judgemental we are, the more room we leave for loving feelings to enter.

The difference between a flower and
a weed is a judgement.
ANONYMOUS

Whenever we pass judgement on people and events, we create barriers which prevents us from having a healthy openness - this makes it more difficult for us to learn from our experiences.

....when you judge, you cut off understanding and
shut down the process of learning to love.
DR. DEEPAK CHOPRA

Loving doesn't mean continuously declaring "I love you", it means to be open and receptive and to ignore superficial irritations or shortcomings. This becomes easier when we try to withhold our judgement and focus instead on a person's inner beauty.

Once we realise that most people are doing things in the best way that they know how, according to the stage of development that they are presently at, we will begin to develop a compassion and love in our hearts which will immensely improve the quality of our own lives.

We shouldn't care about the length of his hair
or the colour of his skin,
don't worry about what shows from without,
but the love that lives within.
RAY STEVENS
(EVERYTHING IS BEAUTIFUL)

The essence of compassion is to realise that everyone is on their own path, and with this compassion, judgement is replaced with love. To state that a person shouldn't be as they are is to lack compassion.

The important thing is not to think much but to love much;
and so do that which best stirs you to love.
SAINT TERESA OF AVILA

In every action you take, the energy carried with the action depends on your intention - if you do what you do with good intention from a position of love, the result is much more likely to be life enhancing. If it is your intention to make someone feel good - healthier, happier and more at peace, then your energy will flow freely. **Love and compassion connect us with others; judgement and condemnation tend to separate us.**

It is love that creates, builds,
harmonises and heals.
PAUL LAMBILLION.

Energy flows freely through the body when you are in a state of love, compassion and forgiveness. This is why long held resentments can often lead to chronic disease conditions - it is because the vital energy becomes quashed or mis-directed.

Our feelings also have an influence on our energy field which can be felt on a subtle level by those around us. An energy interchange occurs during our interactions with all living things, so if we maintain feelings of love and goodwill our energy will provide healing everywhere we go. If there are bad feelings present then an energy interchange still occurs but it will not be conducive to healing. How good others feel in our company depends on how "healed" we are. **If we are filled with life, love, energy and vitality then that is the way we will move others to feel in our presence.**

Cultivate great friendliness and
great compassion towards all that lives.
THE BUDDHA.

A spiritual person radiates a special energy - not only by their behaviour, but also by their presence - which has a positive effect on everyone with whom they interact. In this way, they can touch the lives of people with whom they have no direct contact at all, enabling their goodness to spread out in ever increasing circles.

.....if there is one holy person in a village,
the whole village reaps the benefit of his or her enlightenment.
JAMES REDFIELD/CAROL ADRIENNE.

LOVE AND CONNECTEDNESS

Have you ever woken up in the morning and looked with dread at the day ahead? Have you ever sat in a park not noticing the beauty around you because you are thinking about how tough life is? Have you ever waited for a bus feeling fed up with everything or driven along in your car thinking about all the injustices in the world? Have you ever laid awake at night thinking about all the nasty things that have been said or done to you or felt resentment for other people's behaviour towards you? All these thoughts and feelings separate or disconnect us from life and nature and leave us feeling empty and drained of energy.

The energy balance in our body, often called *vital energy,* (or *Chi* in traditional Chinese medicine, or *prana* in Ayurvedic medicine), is the main factor that determines our health. Our level of vitality is affected not only by our diet and lifestyle but also by our thoughts and feelings which also influence our relationships with other people and with nature. If we can maintain good thoughts and feelings during every interaction in life then we will become more connected to the ultimate source of energy and feel filled with life and vitality. **The way to feel truly alive is to genuinely love life.** Often the people who suffer from the greatest lack of energy are those who see life as a waste of time, hate people and the world and have a negative view of everything that happens to them, these people also tend to age and die more quickly.

Love life as you love your child,
your parent, your friend, your lover
and there will be no dream that cannot be pursued, nothing
hidden that you do not have the means to find.
ANDREA PHOTIOU

The more we can see beauty in life, the more energy we will receive from it - love is the primary way to enhance our energy. If you have a scientific education, as I have, this statement may sound a bit far-fetched to you, after all, isn't our energy level governed by life-style and diet? This is the orthodox view, but I believe that feeling love really can enhance our energy. This occurs on two levels:

1) Your love for life will affect your own internal state and so your whole physiology will adjust so that energy flows through the body more freely, in other words *your vitality increases*.

2) You are an interacting system with your environment, so the more connected you are with it, the more you will receive energy from it. True love is synonymous with connection.

I am not referring to romantic love although this may, occasionally, be included, I am talking here about the love which comes from seeing the beauty within people and nature. This appreciation of the intrinsic beauty of life is very different to the type of appreciation of beauty as seen through the eye of the critic or even through the eye of the artist - true appreciation of beauty comes when there is no thought, no judgement or no philosophical contemplation whatsoever. It is wrong to think that we can't have awareness without thought, since some of the most profound and pure states of awareness come when we are free from thought. I believe that the view that we can't have awareness without thought has come about due to the confusion between these two distinct, but almost undefinable processes - "thought" and "consciousness".

The aim is to experience beauty, not *to think about* experiencing beauty. For some this may come automatically and spontaneously, but for others it takes time, which may, initially, require a conscious decision to feel good feelings towards everyone and everything in life. In other words, before you can *feel* that you love life, you may first need to *think* that you love life. This is true of most emotions, not only love - if you first *think* about the feeling, you may later *feel* the feeling. If you start off *thinking* life is tough, you will, within a very short time, begin to *feel* that life is tough. So, it is really your feelings rather than your thoughts that effect your internal state. However, having said that, since nearly every thought is accompanied by a feeling, it is still true to say that *you are what you think.*

Once you can get to feel good feelings towards everyone and everything in life, a connection is made with nature which is more than just a feeling - this is true love.

> *The essence of love isn't a feeling*
> *- it is a state of being.*
> DR. DEEPAK CHOPRA

Some claim that once this connection has been made with nature it is no longer necessary to consume food for our energy needs, since we can extract all the energy we need directly from the universe. However, this suggestion is going a bit too far for any of us educated (or brain-washed) with the modern, western, scientific, mechanistic view of the universe.

If you see the world through a traditional scientific framework, you may say that *the feeling* that you are receiving energy is *only a feeling* and that there isn't *really* an actual flow of energy just because you love something. However, people who can see the aura around people and nature say that if they observe someone who is in the process of appreciating the immense natural beauty of, say, a landscape, they can actually observe a flow of energy from the environment into the person who is in the process of appreciating nature. It is as if the process of loving sets up an energy flow between the source and the object of love.

If you genuinely love
or at least send kind thoughts to a thing,
it will change before your eyes.
JOHN AND LYN ST. CLAIR THOMAS

Experiment with this. Next time that you are in a social situation, make it your intention to transmit good feelings and loving energy to those around you - you may be surprised at the results.

ROMANTIC LOVE

If we seek to be loved,
if we expect to be loved,
this cannot be accomplished;
We will be dependent and grasping, not genuinely loving.
M. SCOTT PECK, M.D.

To truly love someone, we need to appreciate the intrinsic beauty within them, without asking for anything in return and without setting any conditions. This is often referred to as unconditional love and it is very rare indeed in romantic relationships.

Whenever we *truly* connect to someone and feel a genuine, (non-romantic) love in our heart, we grow a little - when we *truly* love someone, the connection creates a flow of energy which enhances the well-being of both parties. This view of love as a connective energy is in enormous contrast to the traditional western view of love which is more often associated with want, need, desire, lust, jealousy, possessiveness, and so on. These negative characteristics demonstrate that there is an absence of love and arise due to inner insecurities and feelings of self-doubt, which give rise to a kind of ego motivated need to be loved.

Love is patient and kind, it is not jealous or proud.
Love is not selfish or irritable
and does not keep a record of wrongs.
Love never gives up and it's faith, hope and patience
never fail. True love is eternal.
1 CORINTHIANS 13, 1 - 8

The mistake that many of us make when we "fall in love" is to think that our joy and love *comes from* the other person, rather than realising it comes from within us.

Consider two people: one who is "in love" with life and gets pleasure from breathing the air, eating a meal, looking at a flower, and so on, and another who feels totally fed-up with life. Now, if each of these two people meet someone and fall in love, they will both feel a great boost of energy and enthusiasm for life. However, the first person will be able to love in a much healthier way since they will not be clinging on to their partner for fear of losing this wonderful feeling.

Healthy relationships are based not on neediness but
on the passion and excitement of sharing the
journey into becoming a whole person.
SHAKTI GAWAIN

A possessive, clingy type of love (which often, isn't love at all) usually comes from an intrinsic insecurity and fear of loss. This type of clingy love can sometimes repel the person who is the focus of this needy feeling; it also creates dissatisfaction within the needy person. This is in great contrast to someone who feels okay within themselves and subsequently meets someone who they can appreciate for who they really are.

Love one another but make not a bond of love.
Let there be spaces in your togetherness.
KAHLIL GIBRAN

If we want only to possess, then we do not truly love since the feeling is for ourselves and not for the other person. But, unconditional love can only occur between two emotionally balanced people who have sorted out all of their own psychological and emotional baggage and who do not have the need for anyone in their life to make them feel more complete.

The more space you allow
and encourage within a relationship,
the more the relationship will flourish.
DR. WAYNE W. DYER

A relationship is heading for failure if two people get together solely for the reason that something is missing in their life, and there is a desperate need for someone to make their life more complete, since, if this is the case, they are looking not to give but to receive. If, in this situation, someone is successful in their search for a partner, they will think that they have found love but in reality it is just the temporary satisfaction of the need to feel whole. If someone is looking for love due to a feeling of not being whole and complete, then they are looking not for love but for something which can fill a gap in their life.

The arithmetic of love is unique:
Two halves do not make a whole;
only two wholes make a whole.
JO COUDERT

If we *need* someone for our emotional well-being and stability the relationship won't be as healthy as if we don't need them.

Any long-term relationship which is based on this type of needy love, may, very often, start to go downhill as soon as the initial passion has worn off. This is because a relationship based on need rather than love nearly always leads to control and manipulation problems. The only way that we can be in a position to not *need* someone's love, is if we already have love in our hearts - that is, if we feel a love for ourselves and for all of life. In this way we won't need to form a romantic relationship to make us feel "alive" since we will already feel whole when we are on our own. **The greatest feeling of freedom in life comes when we are able to let go of those we love, rather than cling onto them.**

When you set others free, you set yourself free;
when you cling onto others, you hold yourself in a trap.

For an emotionally insecure couple who are "in love" and decide to make their relationship more permanent by living together or getting married, the downward slope to divorce or separation usually takes approximately one to two years. But, with awareness, this needn't be the case and many relationship problems diminish considerably once we develop the awareness that problems often come about not by another's "difficult" behaviour, but due to our own need to be in control.

Many relationships break down because the attitude that each person takes is one of *"you scratch my back and I'll scratch yours"* as opposed to *"what can I give to this person to enhance their life?"* Each individual then continually checks that they are getting as much from the relationship as they are giving to it. If someone has this attitude, anger and resentment inevitably arise which ultimately leads to conflict. In any relationship, it is essential to sometimes ask yourself: "Am I in this relationship so that this person can give me what I need, or would I still love them even if they were no longer with me?

If love does not know how to give and take
without restrictions, it is not love, but a transaction.
EMMA GOLDMAN

You will be truly amazed at how much richer your relationships can become if you focus your attention on what you can give rather than on what you can receive in any relationship. **When we can learn to love without conditions, we will create miraculous relationships.**

Truly wedded are those that
in two frames, are as one light.
SIKHE PROVERB.

The kind of bond that forms when two people love each other unconditionally is only possible when there is a deep sense of trust, this can only come when there is total openness and honesty going in both directions.

Love that is based on mutual understanding
and respect will never drain us of our resources;
our fund of love is replenished even as it flows out of us,
as though the act of loving generates more love.
KAREN CASEY / MARTHA VANCEBURG

The healthiest relationship between a couple who are still in the process of adapting to each other, is one where both partners are not trying to change the other, but instead are working on themselves - they can then give and receive love from each other while developing to a stage where they might learn to love unconditionally.

There is no difficulty that enough love will not conquer;
No disease that enough love will not heal;
No door that enough love will not open;
No gulf that enough love will not bridge;
No wall that enough love will not throw down;
No sin that enough love will not redeem...........
.....If only you could love enough you would be
the happiest and most powerful being in the world.
EMMETT FOX

RESOLVING CONFLICT

The best victory is the one in which everyone wins.
TERRY DOBSON/VICTOR MILLER

Throughout history there has been conflict within relationships through one individual telling another that he or she must change. When two people argue, if each individual thinks that they themselves are right, and each person shirks the responsibility that they may have in creating the conflict by putting the blame on to the other person - the result is inevitable - a stalemate with no winners. It is ironic to consider that this no-win situation comes about because both want to win. The only way that this situation can be resolved is if each individual works on the way that they themselves need to change, instead of focusing on the faults of the other person.

If, after looking at a situation of domestic conflict, you still insist "No, *he is* totally to blame, it is *all* his fault" then maybe the next challenge is to look within yourself not for how you are *causing* the problem but possibly how you are *perpetuating* it, or even how you might be promoting the behaviour of the other person because of the way you relate to them. Remember, your life is a product of your consciousness.

People are slowly waking up to the fact that a positive transformation occurs *only* if each individual works on themselves. If each member of a couple is always wanting the other to change it will always lead to conflict, this is for several reasons, a few of which are:

1)   It is impossible to change someone else unless they also want to change.

2)   Putting blame onto someone creates hostility and sets up barriers.

3)   Judgement stops the flow of love.

4)   If you "pay attention" to someone's negative qualities then it is their negative qualities that will develop.

Our ego always tries to justify our own point of view as "right" and the other person's as "wrong". Most human beings suffer from this self-sabotaging condition which very rarely leads to positive consequences. This "I am right, you are wrong" syndrome is what leads to most of the conflict, animosity, hostility and division on this planet. But with awareness this can be transcended. If *both* individuals try to look at a situation of conflict from the other's point of view and take their share of the responsibility in the creation or perpetuation of the argument then a solution can be found, which could lead to two winners. In other words endeavour to live as if *you really are responsible.*

Feeling that you are always right will not help to resolve a conflict. In any argument, you must ask yourself what you want more: do you want to prove yourself right or do you want to establish a situation of peace and harmony?

In our society it is generally accepted that we can only win if we make someone else lose - this is often taken to its extreme and instead of someone working on their own development to try and win, they spend all their time and energy on trying to make their competition worse off. This is a very sad state of affairs and is most clearly demonstrated in politics where a particular party will spend considerable time and energy not on expressing all the good that they can do, but instead, on expounding what a mess their opposition is making. This "competitive mentality", generated by the ego, requires that in order to feel uplifted we must put somebody else down.

It is important to learn to communicate in a complimentary, up-lifting and encouraging way. Try to point out a person's good qualities while helping them to become aware of what they need to work on. But be sure to distinguish between "helping them to become aware of what they need to work on" and "trying to make them change". If we communicate by criticising, blaming, patronising, (or even worse by ridicule and humiliation) then the results will never be positive.

If we can remain in a state of love,
we will be beyond judgement, blame or aggression.

If you are expecting your partner to change in order for you to love them more, then this is not really love but a feeling based on conditions. A far more responsible and self-empowering stance would be to look at their behaviour as giving you an opportunity to learn unconditional love and acceptance.

A common technique to avoid the impulsive reaction is to internally count to ten before responding. The important thing here is to put a delay in your response so that during this delay, awareness can be present so that a more conscious response can take the place of the reaction. Remember this next time someone says something that makes you feel angry or irritated, instead of responding impulsively to create or perpetuate an unpleasant situation just practice remaining silent. However, this is easier said than done - for most of us it requires a considerable amount of work.

Although, for most of us, it is indeed a great challenge to feel love in the face of conflict, if we can begin by taking this first step then within the silence we will gain various benefits. Firstly, we will feel a relief in having side-stepped a battle which will give us space to observe the other person in a clearer light. Secondly, we will be giving ourselves time to try to understand why the conflict is occurring. Finally, we allow the other person to hear only their own voice, and in so doing, give them a chance to listen to themselves.

What we really need to discover is to find a way to win in life, without making our opposition lose. The only way that this can be achieved is if we no longer see others as our "opposition" but instead see them as our partners, friends and colleagues. We would live much more successfully if we could base all our actions on co-operation rather than competition, but to achieve this we must be motivated not by rivalry, aggression, and the need to control, but by love, compassion and understanding.

Man must evolve for all human conflict,
a method which rejects revenge, aggression and retaliation.
The foundation of such a method is love.
MARTIN LUTHER KING

One of the main keys to avoiding conflict is to practice listening without judgement. In a tense situation of domestic conflict, such as verbal provocation by a family member or marriage partner, the best response would be to take a deep breath and hold an inner smile, rather than to "react" in an aggressive manner.

If someone throws something negative at us, it is totally natural to *react* with negativity, however this can create a perpetuating avalanche of negativity which we can only avoid if we are able to *respond* with awareness. When we refuse to retaliate in the face of conflict, we begin to take control. **The best weapon that we can use against strong, insistent aggression, is strong, insistent kindness** - but this needs considerable inner strength and the clear awareness and conviction from the heart that this is the correct way forward.

> *Don't see being kind and considerate*
> *in the face of conflict as a weakness,*
> *even if that is how it appears to others.*
> *Instead, know it as a sign of great strength.*
> ANDREA PHOTIOU

KEEPING QUIET TO AVOID CONFLICT

Within any relationship, keeping secrets has the effect of diminishing the bond between the individuals concerned. Keeping quiet to avoid arguments causes an inner festering, which, on a long-term basis, is not healthy and will eventually manifest in some way or another.

> *Each time we draw back from potential conflict,*
> *each time we choose silence or conciliation*
> *rather then expressing what is true*
> *for us, we die a little.*
> MALCOLM STERN /SUJATA BRISTOW.

With truthfulness and a clear communication, devoid of any secrets, a much greater intimacy can be attained, and with this openness our relationships with others can develop to a much more meaningful level.

In many relationships, certain topics of conversation always seem to lead to arguments; the usual response to this is to simply avoid the subject in question and to keep your opinions or your feelings to yourself. Whether or not this has undesirable consequences depends on any negative feelings such as resentment being held, due to the withholding of the information. There is, however, a balance that can be struck between expressing oneself to avoid a build up of resentment, and avoiding *unnecessary* conflict by expressing that which is unnecessary to express. In which case we must ask the question: when does keeping quiet become dishonesty?

It is true that even honesty has its discretionary boundaries. If being "economical with the truth" is less disturbing to a relationship than telling the whole truth then this may sometimes be justified. However, if dishonesty becomes a way of life to continually avoid discord, then barriers and bridges will be created that may eventually become insurmountable and the quality of the relationship will inevitably diminish.

There are two conditions which need to be satisfied in order for us to be totally open with someone: we need to feel good about who we are and we need to feel *safe* with the person with whom we are communicating. For real honesty to exist it is not only necessary to have acceptance for ourselves but also to feel *safe* with the other person. I emphasise the word 'safe' because this is a very important factor that determines the level of love present in a relationship.

Safe, means to feel that one's personality, beliefs, and, most of all, short-comings, are not going to be mocked or ridiculed by the other person. When this is the case we are more likely to apologise for our short-comings, whereas if we feel unsafe with someone we may become defensive - defending our short-comings - and therefore inadvertently nurturing them, (remember, where attention goes, energy flows).

However, this defensive barrier that we set up to protect our emotions will not only inadvertently nurture our short-comings, but also repress our positive qualities and emotions. So, the person who is intolerant and critical will lose out on the two things that love thrives on - the expression of a person's qualities and the healthy emotions that thrive when openness and acceptance are present. If two people don't feel safe with each other, a rift develops which blocks communication and love, it then doesn't matter how comfortable we are with our own short-comings, we will still find a barrier when we try to approach the other person.

You may be thinking to yourself now, as you read this, "So the problems I am having in my relationship are not my fault, *I am not responsible,* it is all my partners fault because they don't make me feel safe". However, the problem lies not in the inclination to cover up or be dishonest but in the relationship itself, and in the obvious insecurities, doubts and fears that exist in either or both parties. In a situation of conflict, it may be particularly difficult to accept that, as much as we may want to, we cannot change another, only ourselves and our own attitude and approach. If we don't feel safe with another, we can still take some of the responsibility for the other person not giving out signals of safety and acceptance, and ask ourselves in what way we may have created this inharmonious interaction. If someone is attacking our short-comings it is a very natural response to attack theirs in return. Dishonesty is a *symptom* of discord - the real reason lies elsewhere. Often it is created by an apparent incompatibility due to differences of opinion. This, however, will only lead to conflict if there is an associated power struggle due to each ego wanting to exert its own influence and control. If a couple can work together side by side, respecting each others differences rather than fighting them, then the differing beliefs can bring balance into a relationship rather than producing conflict. The exciting challenge that we may face is to practice loving, or at least accepting, the different views of another rather than fighting and resisting them and hence producing conflict.

The Path
To Happiness

THE PATH TO HAPPINESS

I would like, at the outset, to point out the distinction between happiness and pleasure. Many people think that if they satisfy their desires then they will be happy, but this is generally not true and whilst they may experience moments of pleasure it will not usually lead them any closer to a state of happiness. The most obvious example is sex - good sex will always give pleasure, but whether it leads to happiness depends on a multitude of other factors including love for our partner, inner peace, how emotionally secure we are, and previous conditioning about sex. The same is true of all types of "entertainment" - sensory stimulation attracts us and also distracts us from our inner turmoil, but usually fails to bring us any closer to a state of lasting happiness.

FIRST LOOK WITHIN

Most of us at some point experience states of mind such as worry, fear, hate, resentment, depression, self-pity, and so on, that keep us from experiencing inner peace. Putting our attention on this inner negativity then creates an inner turmoil which considerably brings down the quality of life. The contents of our mind is clearly just as important, if not more important, than external circumstances in determining how we feel in any moment.

Happiness is an internal state created
when you are at peace with yourself and the world
and accept things as they are.

Many people while in a state of inner turmoil just put on the television or radio to distract themselves from what they are really feeling. If we do this we may forget our inner turmoil for a short while, but as soon as the distraction disappears the awareness of the negative state comes back with full force. What we ideally need to do is learn to resolve the inner turmoil while recognising outside activities for what they are - temporary distractions.

*True happiness is found when
you have a peaceful mind and a loving heart.*

Repressing, ignoring or hiding our inner turmoil by distracting ourselves with activities or entertainments is, in some ways, similar to someone who is smelly and unwashed and instead of having a bath they just put on a strong perfume to cover the smell. If we first deal with our emotional baggage, or have a thorough "emotional cleanse", all other experiences will become much more valuable and enriching. Before we bring in the new we've got to clear out the old. Within western culture, sensory stimulation as an entertainment is often used in the hope that it will bring happiness, whereas in practice the reverse is usually true. The sensory stimulation acts as a distraction which "suppresses the symptoms" and therefore stops us dealing with the things we need to deal with in order for us to become healthy, happy and peaceful. This is exactly analogous to the problems caused by orthodox medicine which may prescribe pain killers when we have a pain, fever suppressants when we have a fever, or anti-inflammatory drugs when there is inflammation. It is *always* far better if we can find the cause and deal with that rather than suppress the symptoms, since, when we do this, the problem is bound to manifest in some other way. The Naturopathic view of disease is that all chronic illnesses are the result of continually suppressing (or ignoring) acute conditions.

In a similar way, unhealthy states of mind can arise or get worse when we suppress them by external distraction or by running away from our problems instead of dealing with them.

FINDING INNER PEACE

Make peace with yourself and heaven and earth
will make peace with you.
ST. ISAAK OF SYRIA

You are more likely to respond to others in a peaceful way when you are feeling inner peace within you. To establish a sense of peace within you, it is an essential requirement to feel happy in your own company. This comes about when you feel good about yourself. If you can't find inner harmony while you are just sitting quietly alone then you will find it difficult to find true peace in any other situation. **To find peace and harmony outside of ourselves, we must first find it within.**

You won't find your heart in a temple,
if you don't have a temple in your heart.
DR. WAYNE W. DYER

Some people take more than half a life-time to realise that happiness is an internal state, and even though it is often tempting to say: "If I had this then I would be happy" it is by looking inside and not outside that we will each find our path to true happiness.

For the root to be out of order and the
branches to be in order is an impossibility.
CONFUCIUS

Some people ask: "What right have I to be happy when there is so much suffering in the world?" I think that a much more valid question is: "What right have I to be miserable and increase the suffering in the world, when there is so much already?" It is clear that we won't find true happiness if all our aims are self-centred, but being miserable about all the misery in the world won't help anyone, unless we use our feelings, such as anger about injustice, to motivate us to do something to improve the situation.

If our aim in life is to help alleviate some of the suffering in the world, it is important to realise that we don't necessarily need to travel across the world to achieve this, we can start just where we are by having the intention to help, in whatever way we can, everyone that we interact with in our lives. We will have much more chance of creating good feelings in others if we radiate joy and happiness with a smiling face, than if we radiate misery and discontentment. If we go through life with the intention of helping promote happiness, we cannot fail to contribute, at least a little, to the amount of happiness in the world.

> *Happiness is a by-product of an effort*
> *to make someone else happy.*
> GRETTA BROOKER PALMER

It is clear that the truest feelings of happiness come, not when we are receiving but when we are giving. The following poem by Helen Steiner Rice, describes in a wonderful way that happiness comes more from trying to make others happy than by living in a self-centred or egocentric way:

> *Everybody, everywhere seeks happiness it's true,*
> *but finding it and keeping it seems difficult to do.*
> *Difficult because we think that happiness is found,*
> *only in the places where wealth and fame abound.*

And so we go on searching in palaces of pleasure,
seeking recognition and monetary treasure,
unaware that happiness is just a state of mind,
within the reach of everyone who takes time to be kind.

For in making others happy, we will be happy too,
for the happiness you give away returns to shine on you.
HELEN STEINER RICE

FLOW WITH LIFE

If anything bad happens, be it an inconvenience or a tragedy, we will suffer until we come to terms with the event. Once we accept what has happened our suffering will diminish. I am using the word "suffer" here to mean any unpleasant internal state such as feeling hurt, miserable, upset, dissatisfied, depressed or fed up.

Acceptance is the key
to freedom from suffering.

Most emotional suffering is caused by an unwillingness to accept things as they are, always wishing things were different - acceptance is essential for inner peace.

Be in harmony with life at all times,
be at peace with the world and
patiently accept life as it is.
THE BUDDHA

Most of the negative states that a human being suffers from come from non-acceptance - wishing events happened differently to how they did, wanting things to be different to how they are, or hoping that things will work out a certain way in the future. I like to compare life to a flowing river, if we trust in life and flow with it everything will seem easier and more pleasant than if we continually struggle against the flow. **To swim with the tide is always easier than to swim against it.**

> *Anyone who flows as life flows,*
> *has solved the enigma of human existence.*
> LAO TZU

This doesn't mean that we should be like a leaf blowing in the breeze, allowing life to blow us this way and that, since we do have free will. However, we must **accept the unchangeable aspects of life** whether good or bad and not keep wishing that things were different to how they are.

A few examples of the type of life events that we must learn to accept are:

1) Any relationship if not nurtured with love will inevitably result in conflict, hostility or indifference.
2) A tidy house can get messy very easily without any effort, but a messy house won't get tidy on its own.
3) Dust accumulates and things become dirty if left alone.
4) Sometimes it's sunny and sometimes it rains.
5) Death is a natural process.
6) Nothing is permanent.

Someone who always resents these natural properties of the universe, or aspects of life, will never find inner peace.

If we can trust that the experiences that happen to us in life are all part of some plan and are not just random, meaningless events, then life can be rich and full of purpose. The fact is that **if we trust in life and develop the view that everything that**

happens to us is for a reason, (even if we can't, at present, figure out what the reason is), and we go with the flow of life rather than against it, then life will become an exciting, meaningful journey.

Life is a series of natural and spontaneous changes.
Don't resist them - that only creates sorrow.

LAO TZU

To get an approximate measure of how quickly you come to terms with minor upsets, inconveniences or even tragedies, think carefully about how long it would take you to come to terms with, and feel acceptance and inner peace about the following situations?

1)   You just finished washing up five minutes ago and there is already a new pile of dirty dishes rapidly accumulating. (It is important to note that often, more energy can be used in feeling fed-up due to seeing the dirty dishes, than is used in washing them!)

2)   You really fancy a glass of milk and just as you get the last bottle out of the fridge it slips out of your hand and breaks.

3)   A job comes up that you have always wanted, but on the day of the interview you are too ill to get up. (If this were to happen, it might be useful to ask yourself the question: "what can I learn from this illness, why has my body become ill now, at this time?)

4)   You have just returned to your car to discover an enormous dent in the side.

5)   Last week you bought a new jacket for £100; you just passed a shop and saw the same jacket for £40.

6)   You arrive home from a wonderful evening out to discover you have been burgled - much of value has gone, but you are insured.

None of the above examples are tragedies, they are mostly the type of inconveniences that can happen at any time. Most of them would produce a response in most people of: "Oh damn it", or perhaps another four letter word! But how long would it take for the feeling to disappear? One minute or six months?

Moving on to more serious "inconveniences", imagine that you have just received a letter telling you that you are being made redundant, would you:

1)   Get depressed thinking about boredom, poverty and hunger.
2)   Worry that you may have trouble getting another job.
3)   Accept it and even get excited about the new opportunities that will open up.

If this event were to actually happen, although it *might* produce some very hard times, you are more likely to have opportunities come up if you can keep a positive, optimistic attitude than if you just sit down and get depressed. Having said that, to pass through a period of denial and depression is totally normal, especially when the loss is great. But life becomes more joyful if we can minimise the time for which we may just repeat to ourselves over and over again "Why did this have to happen to me?" or "If only I did that, then everything might have been different." There is absolutely no benefit in spending weeks or months wishing, regretting or saying: "if only....".

If we have a bad accident which could have been avoided, instead of saying "if only ......", it is more productive to adjust our attitude to one of "Well, it has happened now, I may as well see what I can learn from the experience, put it behind me and carry on with my life." A change in our attitude to deal with any challenging situation is essential for the healing process to progress unimpaired. Remaining positive may be difficult sometimes, but it will help if we can be aware that as human beings we are all equipped to survive. We need to help ourselves by believing in our own strength and resilience rather than putting our attention on hopelessness and resentment.

*Each small pebble, stone, or boulder we come across in life
becomes a personal challenge to be met head on with
all of one's self. Some we will not be able
to move nor ignore. Acceptance can be
the most difficult challenge of all.*
ANDREA PHOTIOU

Some people think that "to accept things as they are" means "not to try and change anything". It does not mean this at all, it is simply saying that we should be at peace with *the nature of things*. Acceptance often requires strength, tolerance and a clear view that embraces the whole situation. If we can accept the universe as it is, meaning every aspect of life, then we can truly find inner peace.

*Do not grieve over the inevitable;
everything is as it should be.*

If we can't accept the way things are then we are said to be in denial. Being in denial stops us from attaining happiness and peace of mind because it puts us in a constant state of resistance. If we are in denial we will feel heavy and constantly miserable but when we have acceptance and flow with life we become light and unburdened.

When we cling to pain
we end up punishing ourselves.
LEO F. BUSCAGLIA

It is not only bad experiences and emotional pain that we have to accept, for many people the greatest challenge of all is to accept the impermanence of the pleasurable things in life - this too is something that we need to develop acceptance for.

We have all, at some point, seen children who get into a tantrum when they are having a wonderful time and then that good time comes to an end. But as they mature they slowly learn that they must come to terms with the fact that nothing is permanent. Most adults would recognise the immaturity in a child who cries whenever they have to go home after an enjoyable evening out. However, there are many adults who, although they may not cry, they still haven't learnt a mature, healthy acceptance of the way things are and must be. They may go on holiday, have a wonderful time and then get depressed when the holiday comes to an end. It is then important to ask the question: "What was the point of having the good time?" If the result of going on holiday is sadness or depression, it seems that it was hardly worth going! The cause of the sorrow was obviously not the holiday, it was *non-acceptance of the way things are.* "Oh, why do good times always have to end?", "Why can't this holiday last forever?", "Why does life have to be like this?". Unless we can have total acceptance then we are all, in certain respects, like those screaming children.

All good things must have an end.
PROVERB

In some ways, life can be seen as one big holiday. One of the main factors that stop many people from seeing things in this way is the impermanence of life and the fact that one day this holiday is going to come to an end! What a sad situation if the main thing that stops us enjoying this holiday called life is the fact that one day it's going to come to an end - especially since life has millions of moments, but death has but one.

With acceptance life can be so rich: no worries about the future because we trust in life and we know deep in our hearts that everything that it offers us is for a reason; no regrets, to keep us dwelling in the mistakes of the past; no fear to spoil the moment because we trust that we will have the strength to deal with whatever situation presents itself to us in the future.

Even though life sometimes *seems* unfair from our limited, restricted viewpoints, many spiritual teachers have tried to teach us the fact that life has its own natural balance, and it is, in essence, fair when seen from a more panoramic viewpoint.

> *Things that appear random to a limited awareness fit into place perfectly when awareness is expanded.*
> DR DEEPAK CHOPRA

As we evolve in consciousness, we see more clearly the reasons why things happen the way they do. The following poem expresses in a wonderful way that the universe is perfect - it is as it should be - despite the fact that we generally don't realise it due to our human limitations.

> *All nature is but art unknown to thee;*
> *All chance, direction which thou cannot see;*
> *All discord, harmony not understood;*
> *All partial evil, universal good;*
> *And, spite of pride, in erring reason's spite;*
> *One truth is clear, whatever is, is right.*
> ALEXANDER POPE

The following prayer encompasses most of the ideas of this section. It is very well-known in religious circles and has come to be known as "The Serenity Prayer":

God, grant me:
The serenity to accept the things I cannot change;
the courage to change the things I can,
and the wisdom to know the difference.

REINHOLD NEIBUHR

LEARN TO FORGIVE

Forgiveness is the most powerful
thing you can do to get on the spiritual path.
If you can't do it you can forget about getting to higher levels
of awareness and creating real magic in your life.

DR. WAYNE W. DYER

The word *resentment* means to retain negative feelings for someone after we feel that they have hurt us. If we feel anger and resentment towards someone because our unfortunate situation is *"all their fault"* then the climb out of the unpleasant situation will be a difficult one. The ability to forgive goes hand in hand with the ability to take responsibility for our own feelings. As soon as we can forgive and let go of any resentment, we will feel an immediate freedom from the bondage caused by our negative feelings.

He who cannot forgive others breaks the bridge
over which he himself must pass one day.

PROVERB

If we hold a grudge towards someone, it reflects back on us, and causes more harm to ourselves than to the person that it is focused on. It is difficult to love someone whom we can't forgive, since resentment stops the flow of love, and causes hostility and anger which only serve to separate us from them. If this happens in a relationship it can't survive. So, if we feel resentment and anger towards someone, we could either, express those feelings to relieve the internal tension that they may cause, or work on ourselves with the intention of letting go of the negative feelings.

Anger repressed can poison a relationship
as surely as the cruellest words.
JOYCE BROTHERS

If what we need to forgive is someone else's abusive behaviour towards us, this does not mean to accept that it is okay. Remember, the serenity prayer says *accept what you can't change, but change what you can.* In this particular case it is not a matter of trying to change the abuser since this creates hostility which can lead to more abuse. The empowered, responsible person looks at how, through their own behaviour, they are either creating, promoting, or at the very least, allowing the abuse to take place. One of the fantastic consequences of forgiving another is that as you release resentments and expand your own consciousness, your life changes to correspond to this. The abuse will then cease automatically.

If you find it difficult to forgive someone who hurt you in a situation of marital, family or social conflict, then it can help considerably if you keep in mind that they were also victims at some level, and that they were behaving according to the level of consciousness from which they were functioning at that time. To have compassion means to realise that **everyone is entitled to be as they are, including you.**

We are all doing the best that we can according to our present level of consciousness.

Probably the greatest challenge of all is to forgive someone who committed a violent or unjust act against us. In this case it may help to consider that they were also victims at some point in their lives and were themselves acting out of an inability to forgive those who hurt them.

Inner peace can be reached only when we practice forgiveness.
GERALD G. JAMPOLSKY

Resentment often arises due to someone behaving in a way that *we consider* wrong, unfair, hurtful or nasty. But sometimes it may simply be due to their behaviour being different to "an ideal response" that we may have hoped for; if this is the case then, what might be required is not for the person to change their behaviour, but for us to change our image of what their behaviour should be. If we don't have any expectations from a person then resentment is less likely to arise.

Be tolerant with each other and have forgiveness. And to these qualities add love, which binds all things together in perfect unity.
COLOSSIANS 3, 12 - 14

There is no greater virtue than the ability to forgive your enemy. Speaking words of love to someone or about someone immediately begins to dissipate the negative emotions that may be present.

Forgiveness heals all ills.
Forgiveness makes the weak strong.
Forgiveness makes the mournful happy.
Forgiveness makes the ignorant wise.
CATHERINE PONDER

The intention is not to forget, or even worse, to repress painful or unjust experiences; the aim is to let go of self-destructive feelings of resentment, bitterness and blame. Life presents us with experiences so that we can learn something, and then somehow develop towards greater levels of awareness.

The stupid neither forgive nor forget;
the naive forgive and forget;
the wise forgive but do not forget.
THOMAS SZASZ

If someone in your past has been malicious and caused you much misery, it may be very difficult to forgive them, especially if you have held onto that resentment for a long time. Usually this resentment will result in wanting to get your own back on them and see them punished for their actions towards you. To feel vengeful if someone has done you an injustice is totally natural and normal, but it is a very self-destructive emotion which we can recover from only when we are ready to release it with compassion and forgiveness. To actually take revenge is almost always damaging to everyone involved. It is said that revenge is sweet, but in reality it is almost always very bitter indeed.

An eye for an eye, a tooth for a tooth......
......and that way the whole world will be blind and toothless.
ADAPTED PROVERB
(FROM *FIDDLER ON THE ROOF*).

Wanting to see another punished is far more damaging to yourself than to them. If you strive to get even, then you are in a no-win situation. It is far healthier to forgive, and to realise that as long as people continue to be malicious and cause misery to others they can never be happy, and this in itself is life's own punishment.

How we direct our desire, and
whether we join it to our love or our anger,
determines the effect it will have in our lives.
KAREN CASEY / MARTHA VANCEBURG

DON'T FEEL GUILTY

And what about self-forgiveness? If in our lives we have committed a wrong that we regret, then we may feel guilt, remorse or shame, but these are very destructive emotions. Guilt has very damaging effects, both on our personal growth and on our relationships. One of the many harmful consequences of feeling guilt is that it leads to secrecy, causing someone to feel that they can't be totally open about themselves, this, in turn, causes a certain emotional isolation. I am not talking here about the type of guilt which our conditioning may have created, such as eating a cream cake while on a diet, or having sex before marriage. To feel guilty in these instances is totally self-destructive and pointless. In life, there is absolutely nothing wrong with engaging in activities that give pleasure - what we need to avoid is over-indulgence in pleasurable activities - but this is another subject.

What I want to focus on here is the type of guilt that comes from committing acts which have caused harm to others. Even in these instances, guilt seems to be a very self-destructive emotion. Is there any point to it? There is indeed a good reason why the feeling of guilt arises, and it is for the following reason. If someone behaves badly they have two choices, either they can feel okay about it, taking the attitude "I know I was bad, but I don't care" which means that they then have to acknowledge that they are a bad person. Alternatively, they can feel guilty - this feeling of guilt helps them to hold onto the belief that they really are a good person. Neither of these choices are very constructive and there is a third alternative: **The effect of a wrong can be neutralised by acts of kindness.** If you have committed a wrong which you cannot right, it is not worth living each day carrying the burden of guilt, instead you could strive to live your life from this moment onwards being good in every interaction.

*To carry the burden of guilt
neither helps yourself nor anyone else.
Forgive yourself and strive to be kind and
considerate in all your interactions.*

Once we have awareness of what we have been doing wrong then we will be able to begin to make the changes necessary for our well-being and happiness. Guilt is neither helpful nor necessary in this process. If we let go of any feelings of guilt and earnestly try, from this moment on, to endeavour to never intentionally harm any living creature, then it will be easy to have a clean conscience.

A clean conscience is the best pillow.
PROVERB

To have a clean conscience does not require that we have never, ever done anything wrong or brought harm to any living creature. It is much more important what our attention is on in each moment and that we have the intention to enhance the lives of others or improve the planet in some way. Repenting for your sins is of absolutely no benefit unless your actions in the future are different to the actions for which you are repenting. It is of much greater benefit to put your attention on the good that you will do from this moment on, than to focus on the bad that you did in the past.

Just as it is better to avoid judging others, the same is true of ourselves, if we are always criticising ourselves for everything we do, we won't be able to feel good about who we are. The way that some people respond to their own faults or negative characteristics is equivalent to someone who has a broken arm and keeps hitting it because they are so angry that it isn't healthy. Obviously care and nurturing of one's wounds is the way to induce healing - anger and resentment never get us anywhere. If we want to be healthy we *must* forgive.

> *Whenever we are ill, we need to look around*
> *to see who it is that we need to forgive.*
> *A COURSE IN MIRACLES*

ATTITUDES TOWARDS TIME

With nothing to do but expect the hour of setting off,
the afternoon was long.
JANE AUSTEN

Do you ever get irritated when you have to wait for someone? Have you ever been waiting, and during this time had an unpleasant feeling that you are wasting your time? Do you feel that you always have to rush from one place to another? Do you feel that you always have to keep busy going from one job to the next without a pause for breath? Do you find yourself blaming the pace of life today for your hurried attitude?

Whenever you have to make any social arrangements do you always answer: "I just don't have time at the moment" or "I would love to meet you, but I'm too busy", and do you always feel that you are pressured by lack of time while rushing to meet deadlines?

In medicine we realise that people who don't have enough time are going to develop health problems..........
It's no accident that the word deadline
contains the word dead.

DEEPAK CHOPRA

It is very relevant to include this subject in a book about taking responsibility because "time" probably receives more blame for our lives not being as we'd like, than any other factor. But this again, is just a question of attitude, and we play a much greater part than we usually think.

Both waiting and rushing are consequences of the way we look at time. If you are waiting for someone at a station you might be excused for feeling that you are wasting your time if they are late (although this doesn't need to be so), but what about if you are waiting for them at home? Let's suppose that if you weren't waiting you would just be relaxing in your chair listening to some music feeling good. But because you are "waiting" your internal state changes from one of "relaxing and giving yourself to the moment" to one of "anticipation of something to come". It is this *coming out of the moment* that creates the negative effects of both waiting and rushing.

He sows hurry and reaps indigestion.
ROBERT LOUIS STEVENSON

Even if you are waiting at the station, you still don't need to get bored since you have the most incredible tool in the universe at your disposal - your imagination! One of the greatest scientific minds of this century, Albert Einstein, made advances in his general theory of relativity by performing "thought experiments", which he could do anywhere, at any time, and, in fact, he said that he often did his best work while waiting. If, while waiting, you are able to give yourself to the moment, you will never get bored, frustrated or angry while waiting for someone if they are a little late, in fact, you would no longer be "waiting", you would be living.

The negative consequences of waiting and rushing are created by the feeling that as time passes by we are losing it not using it.

"To be run by time" is almost synonymous with "to suffer from stress". You may blame life's pressures, or the pace of life today, but people have been projecting the blame in this way for hundreds or perhaps thousands of years, it is certainly not a new complaint.

I am going to join a Gypsy band to escape from the stresses and strains of modern life.
17TH CENTURY STUDENT

Once you realise that you create your life according to your consciousness and that your time problems are a product of the way you perceive time, you can become more free and easy-going in your social or business arrangements - and find, amazingly, that as you *use* more time, you will *have* more time.

Part of the problem is in our understanding of what time is. Due to a life-time of conditioning we understand time as flowing linearly from the past through the present and towards the future. It is important to be aware that we only see time like this because of the way our society is run - based on plans and arrangements. Living in this western time-keeping civilisation it is very difficult to totally transcend this time consciousness unless we can discard our watches and build our lives around a life-style where we don't make "arrangements", but instead are spontaneous in our activities. This is even more of a challenge when it comes to work. In most cases, the best that we can do is be aware of how time restraints can rule our life and dominate our consciousness, and with this awareness we can begin to transcend it.

The many ways that we can view time can be classified into three main categories:

1)   The nervous, excited way - "I've got so much to do and so little time".

2)   The tired, lethargic way - "It's too late so why bother?"

3)   The peaceful, spiritual way - "I've got all the time in the world".

Each of us can have moods when we are in each of these states but every person is dominated primarily by one of the states in particular.

A person who sees time in the first way is primarily living to "get things done", and all ambitions are centred around *doing* rather than *being*. A person living in this way rarely has time to really connect with people or nature on a deep level because they are too busy doing things. Most of us live like this sometimes, but it is important to realise that in many ways how we are *being* is more important than what we are *doing*. What situation would you prefer to be in at the end of the day when you go to bed:

1)   To be aware of the many things that you have got done and then worry about all the things still to be done tomorrow.

2)   To be aware of the way you have flowed through the day, and have a feeling of peace and contentment and a sense of achievement.

Obviously these two states are not mutually exclusive, but the point that I am trying to make is that many people within western culture put emphasis on success and achievement in terms of external activities rather than attaining a certain inner state of being.

> *Success is as much about*
> *living in peace with our own individuality,*
> *as it is about achieving our goals.*
> ANDREA PHOTIOU.

True achievement is not about getting things done, or keeping busy, for if it was we might be more appropriately called "human doings" rather than "human beings". Real achievement is more about what you can be, not in the way of a label such as doctor, dentist, teacher, scientist, artist, but in the sense of a true state of being - in touch with the real you which is loving, compassionate, kind and generous.

A person who sees time in the second way can't be bothered to do or be anything since there is not enough time or energy. It is this attitude to time that gives rise to apathy and a feeling of helplessness. It is often people with this attitude who may sit slumped in front of the television watching the news saying "why don't *they* do something about it?" This attitude is also a consequence of not only one's view on time, but also an inner lack of confidence and feeling of powerlessness.

If we can avoid getting stuck by focusing all our energy on regrets and resentments based on the dead past, or on desires and expectations based on the imagined future, and simply value the experience of each moment, then we *will* have all the time in the world. Meditation is known to be of enormous value in helping us to change our perception of time. Through the regular practice of meditation our attitude adjusts from one of "hurry, there's not enough time", to "take it easy, we've got all the time in the world."

Regarding the third way, you may argue: "But, I haven't got all the time in the world, I am always so busy that I haven't time to do the things I'd like to do!" It is essential to realise that this is just an attitude towards your reality and not reality itself. The fact is that each of us have twenty four hours in each day and we prioritise the way that we spend that time. So, when we say: "I haven't got time to go out and enjoy myself", what we really mean is: "it is low on my list of priorities to go out and enjoy myself". You may continue: "but life *demands* that I spend my time doing these things, I don't do them because I want to." Well, if you take this stance, it means that you are not taking responsibility for your actions, but instead becoming a victim of your circumstances. If we can replace "I have to.........." with "I choose to........", we will feel, and become, much more empowered, and then discover that we do, after all, have much more control over our lives than we previously thought.

Someone who experiences time as
a scarce commodity that is constantly
slipping away is creating a completely different
personal reality from someone who perceives
that he has all the time in the world.
DEEPAK CHOPRA

LIVING FOR THE FUTURE

It is good to have an end to journey towards;
but it is the journey that matters in the end.
URSULA K. LEGUIN

To feel excited about achieving your goals is fine, you can dream about, or plan for the future, but **don't live for the future.**

While I was at college I had a friend who always said: "I am going to be really happy when I get to university, that is what all this study is for." He wasn't studying his 'A' levels for the pleasure of studying or for the sake of the knowledge itself - his intention was simply to arrive somewhere. When he got to university I asked him if he was happy now and he said: "Well, not really, I need to get out to work. When I finish this degree and get a job, then *I will* be happy." We stayed in touch and when he started work I asked him the same question and his answer didn't surprise me: "I don't feel very happy at the moment because I don't like working for someone else, but I know that I will be *really happy* when I start my own business". And so it goes on.

Yesterday's a memory, tomorrow's still a dream.
And reality lies somewhere in between.
ANDREA PHOTIOU

If you have the ambition to get a degree, then the value in it is obviously not just in receiving the certificate at the end, but in the study, the human interactions and the way you live during the years of study. So, you may set yourself an aim, but when you get on the path towards achieving it, strive to live for the path, and not the destination.

Success is a journey not a destination,
half the fun is just getting there.
GITA BELLIN

Many people spend their lives striving to satisfy their heart's desire, thinking that it will bring them such joy, and then when they eventually achieve what they want it is a bit of an anticlimax.

There are two tragedies in life.
One is to lose your hearts desire.
The other is to gain it.
GEORGE BERNARD SHAW

If we are riding on a bus, it could be just a tedious journey that we have to go through so that we can get to our destination, or it could be looked at in a positive way, enjoying the trip, and then the arrival is just an extra bonus. The same applies to our journey through the day. When we wake up we may be thinking about going to the bathroom; while we are in the bathroom we might be thinking about having breakfast; while we are having breakfast we could be thinking about our journey to work; while we are travelling to work; .... and so on, ad infinitum. Every journey can be looked at in this way - this includes our journey through life (just like my friend from college). If we have the aim to get somewhere in life we must try to enjoy the journey there and not just the attainment. If we have an ambition we must ask ourselves: "Is the ambition more for the attainment or for the path it gives me?"

The value of ambition is not in its attainment but
in the experiences created while on the road to attaining it.

If we set our sights simply on the journey's end we will miss so much along the way. For example, if we have the ambition to walk to India, the attainment (i.e. the arrival) is trivial in comparison to the experiences that we will have on the way.

To travel hopefully is better than to arrive.
SIR JAMES JEANS

This is expressed in yet another beautiful way in the following popular proverb:

Happiness is a road to travel,
not a place to be.

The truth is that if we can't enjoy the journey towards the attainment of the ambition, then the attainment will probably be a bit of an anti-climax.

If you are not a whole person before achieving your ambition,
then you will not spontaneously become a
whole person after achieving it.

I wonder how many people have thought: "When I meet a wonderful partner and get married then I will definitely be happy", but when they later meet someone and get married, the reality may not be as they had hoped. In some ways it is often better to delay the realisation of a dream for as long as possible and savour the pleasure of the anticipation.

Anticipation is better than realisation.
PROVERB

If their relationship is not going well they may wish that they were single again, thinking that, although they didn't appreciate their freedom before, they would now. If the relationship is going well, but still lacking something, they might say "when I have a few children *then I really will* be happy, after the children arrive it then changes to something like "when the children are at school and I have more free time to pursue my career then *I am sure* I will be happy"........this is never ending. The only way we can escape from this perpetual cycle of always living for a future moment is to realise that **there is nothing magical that will come in the future to give us happiness** (apart from, perhaps, this realisation!). **We have everything we need to be happy now, in this moment, all we need to do is learn how to give ourselves to this moment and appreciate what we've got, here and now.**

Are you experiencing, or are you spending most of your time thinking about what you experienced or what you will experience?
RICHARD HITTLEMAN

The richness of the experiences that we live depends upon the attitude that we have while travelling along life's path. If we are not careful it is very easy to miss out on the life that we are now living, while forever making plans for the future.

Life is what happens to you while you're busy making other plans.
JOHN LENNON
(BEAUTIFUL BOY)

It is very easy to become immersed in the activities required to achieve our material ambitions, to be busy, busy, busy, and forget about the simple things in life or even to lose sight of why we are doing what we are doing.

Did you see your children growing up today,
and did you hear the music of their laughter
as they set about to play?
Did you catch the fragrance of those roses in your garden,
does the morning sunlight warm your soul
and brighten up your day?

RAY STEVENS
(MR BUSINESS MAN)

LIVING IN THE PAST

It is not only a preoccupation about the future that can stop us living for the moment - for many people living in the past is the major hurdle, this is a state of mind which can also have the effect of stopping us from appreciating what we have here and now. Remembering wonderful moments in the past and feeling good in this moment while we reminisce is fine, but excessive feelings of nostalgia are not so healthy. To look back at past events is sometimes essential, since it's the only way to learn from our mistakes, but we must try our best to **avoid living in the past.**

Nothing is worth more than this day.
GOETHE

It is of no benefit to look back wishing: "If only those wonderful times would come again", especially since, if we are totally sincere with ourselves we may remember that, at that time, we were probably dreaming about the future. As Gladys Knight so wonderfully expresses it in her song "Try to remember":

101

Why does it seem that the past is always better?
We look back and we think that:
The winters were warmer, the grass was greener,
the skies were bluer, and smiles were bright.
Can it be that it was all so simple then,
or has time rewritten every line?
SCHMICT-JONES

Past experiences and memories of good times that have been, should be viewed as gifts that we have already opened and so belong to us forever, not as experiences that have slipped away from us like sand through our fingers.

BE HAPPY - NOW!

Here and now is all we've got.
THE BUDDHA

It is very easy to live in memories of the past, and dreams about the future, and miss the present altogether, but this is like sleeping through a wonderful party - we need to wake up before the party ends - the magic is here and now, we need search no more.

Paradise is where I am.
VOLTAIRE

All the important lessons in life arrive when we are in the moment - making connection with ourselves, with others, and with life - this is when wisdom comes, not from reading intellectual or philosophical literature, but by simply being fully in the moment, in touch with life and appreciating all we observe.

Life would be so much richer if we could develop the peaceful, spiritual attitude towards time, but how can this be achieved? The key lies in giving our full attention to whatever we are doing in any moment. To appreciate life in the full sense of the word, it is essential that we learn to give ourselves to the moment - this means to live for what we have here and now. This is especially valuable when we are in the company of others. Any interaction with another human being has the most value when both are giving each other full attention. Have you ever spoken to someone while thinking about what you have to do in ten minutes or tomorrow? Many people can sense this as a lack of warmth, you may look cold or distant, or you may, at that moment, appear unappealing or boring to talk to and then they may stop the interaction to move on to someone with whom they can make a better connection. But if, while talking to someone, you can give them your full, undivided attention and be with them one hundred percent, as if, for that moment, there is nowhere else in the world that you would rather be - then you will make a true friend.

Reaching out to find the wonder of the here and now,
hand in hand with one another, time will teach us how.
ANDREA PHOTIOU

TOWARDS A PEACEFUL WORLD

The truest measure of how civilised any society is,
is not in how technologically advanced it is, but in
how much peace and harmony exists within that society.

Societies function by the same principles as individuals, since a society is just a collection of individuals. Just as we create our reality by our expectations, by the way we think and speak, and by how we feel about ourselves, society does the same. So, if the media states that crime is rampant then society must live up to this negative "self-image" and make it true. Some people may disagree with this and say: "If all the newspapers started printing how wonderful society is, it wouldn't stop crime because criminal behaviour is not caused by belief or by what people read in the papers, it is caused by poverty and inadequate social conditions". Well, it is probably true to say that society will always have some level of crime but in the past there have been many poor societies where crime was minimal.

Crime appears worse now because that is what the focus of the media is on, and due to this attention, many crimes are committed which otherwise wouldn't occur. On an individual level this is equivalent to someone who always worries that they are going to argue with their partner - inevitably they do!

I find it obvious that many crimes have been committed due to the fact that those crimes have been "advertised" in the media to such a degree. For example, imagine a crime that hardly exists, being committed by one individual and then appearing in all the papers to such an extent that everyone gets to hear about it. The consequences of this would be that anyone in society who has a dormant potential for that crime could be given the idea to do something that they wouldn't have otherwise thought of, and maybe carry out the crime, due to this media stimulation.

Our society at present is suffering from various problems because it is so much more attuned to the negative than the positive. An example of this is illustrated by the "paedophile complex" that many people in our society have now developed due to the extreme media coverage of sexual abuse of children. The average person, both male and female, no longer feels relaxed to talk to a child in the street, in case someone assumes that they have bad intentions. One teacher recently said to me that if a child falls over in the playground and grazes her arm "I can't give her a cuddle, or kiss it better, even if the child is in need of comfort, just in case someone observing might misinterpret the event". I find this a very sad and unfortunate consequence of "sociological negative suggestions", caused by newspapers over-reporting and sensationalising the negative qualities of our society. Another example is the extreme fear that many people now have to go out at night or let their children play outside even during the day. This is a type of sociological paranoia since when we look at statistics of, for example, child murder, it is the same now as it was one hundred years ago - all that has changed is the media's perception and portrayal of this terrible crime.

There have been several attempts, both in Britain and in America, to set up "good news" newspapers and every attempt has led to failure; this leads us to the inevitable conclusion that people prefer to hear and read about "death and disaster" than about "love and acts of kindness". Isn't this a strange thing? I'm not sure whether it is human nature or a social sickness, however, it is the reality within western society.

A newspaper that always prints bad news is equivalent to an individual always thinking negative thoughts and picturing negative images. The inevitable (although, somewhat over-simplified) conclusion that can be drawn from this is that **news reports of crime perpetuate crime in the same way as our negative thoughts and worries tend to manifest the very thing we dread. On a sociological as well as on an individual level we create what we expect.**

All reporters and journalists know that they sell more newspapers if they exaggerate, sensationalise and even create, horrific stories of crime, injustice and cruelty. It is true that these occurrences are present in our society but not to a fraction of the extent that our newspapers portray. **Every day there are good things**

happening - acts of kindness, people devoting their time to helping others, amazing expressions of love and goodwill, charities and organisations being set up with the aim of helping people. But nobody seems to want to read about these things and so we get an illusion that the world is bad. We are all aware that we are living in a partly troubled world, burdened with tragedies, injustices and natural disasters. But there are possibly a thousand good experiences to every bad experience, a thousand acts of kindness quietly carried out for every bad deed we hear about. In the worst trouble spots the light of human love and kindness prevails and it is up to us to add to it by believing that the world is still beautiful and life can still be wonderful despite everything.

Many people talk about the world as if it is something completely separate from themselves, as if everyone else makes the world the terrible place that it is and that they have no part in it. **Every member of society makes up our society and yet most individuals are good people who look upon society as bad.** But everyday more and more people are waking up to the fact that our world is what we make it. In fact, the world is presently going through a cultural and spiritual transformation in which the "old world view" related to materialism, economics and religious dogma is being replaced by a new paradigm which is based on a more spiritual, ecological and holistic way of living.

Each of us have the response-ability - or ability to respond - to media information in whatever way we choose. We can choose not to buy tabloid newspapers or listen to sensationalised news stories. We can avoid gossiping or talking about "that horror story in the paper this morning". If we feel that there are some real injustices in the world that make us feel angry, we can go out and do something about it, rather than hope someone else does.

How do you get world peace?
You get world peace through inner peace.
If you've got a world full of people who have
inner peace, then you have a peaceful world.

DR. WAYNE W. DYER

Most of the problems of the world arise due to a lack of love and a lack of awareness, this, in turn, is created primarily by ego attachments - the "me and mine" or the "look after number one" syndrome. We need to find a way to slowly release ourselves from attachments to worldly possessions and other labels that we cling on to. Some may argue that it is natural to be "attached" to one's family or those who you love, but I would prefer to use the word devotion here, rather than attachment. There is a very subtle, but important, distinction between devotion and attachment, the main difference being that attachment arises from the ego, whereas devotion is totally unselfish. To be devoted to our family, a particular person, a good cause or even our country, is a wonderful thing. But, to be "attached" implies a kind of egocentric "devotion" to the label of "*my* family", "*my* partner", "*my* political party" or "*my* country" - the consequences of this type of attachment are never wholly positive.

The man, who casting off all,
lives free from attachment, who is free from egoism and from
the feelings that this or that is mine, obtains tranquillity.

BHAGAVAD GITA 2.71

To be devoted to our partner gives rise to respect and trust, whereas attachment gives rise to jealousy and possessiveness. Devotion to a religious system might help us to live in a more spiritual way, whereas attachment to the label "I am a Christian (Muslim, Buddhist, Jew...)" sets up barriers to other religious authorities or belief systems and creates a block to finding true wisdom. To be devoted to your body and appreciate it as the temple of your soul helps you to look after it in a healthy way, whereas to be attached to it gives rise to vanity and a fear of ageing or death. Devotion to our country could give us a good feeling about living in it, and help us to feel happy about paying taxes, whereas an attachment to the label of "*my* country" gives rise to unhealthy nationalistic feelings and racist attitudes.

It is not for him to pride himself for loving his own country, but rather for him to love the whole world. The earth is but one country, and mankind its citizens.
BAHA'I FAITH - GLEANINGS 117

Our identity is often wrapped up in labels - name, religion, occupation, sex, nationality, and so on, but it is important to be aware that these are simply labels that have nothing to do with what, or who, we really are. If we could all transcend the attachment to the label of "my country" and replace it with a devotion for, not only our country, but the whole of humanity, then we would begin to live as if we are just one big family. Imagine the whole planet living in unity - then there could be no wars - you may say I'm a dreamer, but I'm not the only one!

Imagine there's no countries, it isn't hard to do. Nothing to kill or die for, and no religion too. Imagine all the people living life in peace......
JOHN LENNON

As the world evolves, and awareness increases, barriers will slowly break down and the planet will become more united. As this happens the suffering caused by the whole host of racial and

108

social prejudices will diminish within the world - maybe this will come true sooner than we expect.

I have a dream.......
.......that children will be judged on the basis of
the content of their character, not the colour of their skin.
.......I have a dream,
that the brotherhood of man will become a reality in this day.
And with this faith I will go out and carve a tunnel
of hope through the mountain of despair.
With this faith I will go out with you
and transform dark yesterdays into bright tomorrows.
With this faith we will be able to
achieve this new day when all of God's children -
black men and white men,
Jews and Gentiles, Protestants and Catholics,
will be able to join hands and sing with
the Negro in a spiritual abode:
"free at last, free at last, thank God we're free at last".
MARTIN LUTHER KING.
(28/8/63)

ADVICE FOR A HAPPY LIFE

Learn to appreciate everyone and everything in your life - the healthiest attitude is an attitude of gratitude.

As you wake up in the morning visualise yourself as a warm, open, loving person and give thanks for the day ahead.

Practice seeing the inner beauty in everyone that you interact with, everyone has some good within them.

Spend at least 20 minutes a day in meditation or deep relaxation.

Spend time in natural environments appreciating the beauty of everything around you.

Cultivate friendliness and peacefulness towards all that lives.

Be considerate, compassionate and humble in all your interactions.

Try to support, respect, encourage and advise anyone, whenever it is appropriate to do so.

Avoid judging, blaming, condemning, criticising, lying, gossiping, insulting, stealing or engaging in any other activity that causes harm to yourself or others.

Practice forgiveness. Release any resentment that you hold in your heart towards anyone that has hurt you.

When you feel anger, resentment, pain, or any other negative emotion, be aware that you own these feelings and endeavour to release them whenever possible.

Practice using your intuition. Be in harmony with life and nature and listen to the wisdom of your inner voice.

When trying to make a difficult decision ask yourself "will this course of action make me feel closer to myself and others or will it create barriers?"

See difficulties that arise in life not as problems, but as challenges and opportunities for growth.

Practice enjoying your own company, spend some time alone each day.

Take notice of the lessons that are constantly coming up in your life - you can learn something from every experience.

See all living beings on this planet as one, fragmentation and division are the main problems in our outlook towards ourselves, our family and our planetary society.

Try to transcend the narrow viewpoints and attachments which give rise to racism, nationalism and segregation.

Visualise yourself as a great success.

Freely express love - not necessarily in words but in actions.

Hold love in your heart towards yourself and others, feel happy about who you are but without arrogance.

Feel the joy of giving as well as of receiving. Be equally open to both give and receive.

Have an open mind to enhance the flow of information, and an open-heart to enhance the flow of love between you and all of life.

Don't blindly accept; don't blindly reject. Give consideration to everything you hear.

Release any beliefs that aren't serving you.

Feel relaxed and at peace with your sexuality.

Give yourself to the moment. Consciously select the activities to which you will give your attention, and then give them your full attention.

Put energy and enthusiasm into everything you do.

Engage frequently in natural exercise such as walking, running, swimming, gardening, etc.

Pay attention to your body's signals of pain, discomfort and tension. There is a message in them.

Eat plenty of fresh fruit and vegetables every day. Minimise your consumption of highly processed foods.

Only eat as much food as your body needs. Relish it, appreciate it, love it and bless it for the life it gives you.

Practice conscious breathing - take deep breaths with the awareness that the air contains a life-energy or prana that sustains life and enhances your energy.

Work on developing the qualities that you have, don't try to be who you are not.

Have compassion for those who are different to you - everyone is entitled to be where they are.

Keep a sense of humour. Start and end each day with a smile, and try to fit in between as many smiles and laughs as possible.

Live with awareness and be mindful in everything you do.

Have acceptance for the unchangeable properties of life. Life is as it is. You are as you are. Everything in the universe is flowing as it is meant to, don't resist it - simply flow with it.

You are a child of the universe,
no less than the trees and the stars,
you have a right to be here.
And whether or not it is clear to you,
no doubt the universe is unfolding as it should.
MAX EHRMANN

Bibliography

Ageless body, timeless mind - Deepak Chopra. Published by Rider 1993.

The power of positive thinking - Norman Vincent Peale. Published by Cedar books.

Handbook to higher consciousness - Ken Keyes Jr. Published by Loveline books.

The Dynamic Laws of Healing - Catherine Ponder. Published by Devorss & Co.

Feel the fear and do it anyway - Susan Jeffers. Published by Arrow Books Limited.

Living in the Light - Shakti Gawain. Published by Eden Grove Editions.

Staying on the path - Dr. Wayne W. Dyer. Published by Hay House, Inc.

The Celestine Prophecy, An adventure - James Redfield. Published by Bantam books.

The Celestine Prophecy, An experiential guide - James Redfield and Carol Adrienne. Published by Bantam books.

You can have it all - Arnold Patent. Published by Money Mastery Publishing, 1984.

A guide for the advanced soul - Susan Hayward. Published by In-tune books.

The nature of personal reality - Jane Roberts. Published by Prentice Hall, Inc.

The promise of a new day - Karen Casey and Martha Vanceburg. Published by Hazelden Meditation series.

Guide to Yoga meditation - Richard Hittleman. Published by Bantam books.

Yoga - Hari Prasad Shastri. Published by W& G Foyle Ltd.

A Course in Miracles. Published by Foundation for Inner Peace.

The Dawn of change - Eileen Caddy. Published by The Findhorn Press.

God spoke to me - Eileen Caddy. Published by The Findhorn Press.

The courage to love - Malcolm Stern and Sujata Bristow. Published by Piatkus.

The road less travelled - M. Scott Peck. Published by Arrow Books Limited.

About the author

Tycho graduated from university in 1982 with a B.Sc. degree in Physics and Astrophysics. He then went on to become a professional musician and teacher of Guitar, Piano and Bass. In 1988 he obtained an Open University degree in Mathematics and Science and is currently lecturing at Southgate College. The rest of his time is divided between his writing and the running of *The British Centre for Wholistic Health*, and *The National Society for Personal Growth* which he founded in 1997.

After finishing his first degree in 1982 he set off around Europe on a personal pilgrimage that was to become the inspirational springboard for this series of books. During his time abroad, and since, he has extensively studied eastern philosophy including Yoga, Buddhism, and Martial arts comparing the principles of Eastern and Western religions and the various interpretations of the concept of God. His disattachment to any religion or doctrine has given him the scope to freely move among the various teachings with an open but necessarily doubting mind.

His path has led him to seek the universal roots of spirituality, extracting the essence of the many aspects of philosophical teachings and religions in the firm knowledge that each has its own treasures to uncover. His discoveries have led him primarily to acknowledge the relationships between the spirit, the mind, and the body working together in order to reach the highest quality of life.

Tycho's background was based on good conventional family values with encouragement towards individual self-discovery. These foundations created in the author a dual loyalty - a respect for established beliefs, both past and present, and an adventurous spirit, exploring new territory, questioning and probing the fertile terrain of life's secret gardens.

This book is both comprehensive and inspiring, and the reader will doubtless find themselves irresistibly launching out on their own voyage of discovery.

Andrea Photiou.

Tycho is a qualified hypnotherapist, a Reiki practitioner, and an experienced teacher and presenter of courses and workshops. He is an independent health researcher and is also involved in stress counselling, wholistic therapy and Naturopathic healing methods. He was trained as a Scientist and worked as a teacher for several years before pursuing his interest in the power of the mind and researching into the various methods available for releasing human potential. The founder and director of *The National Society for Personal Growth* and *The British Centre for Wholistic Health,* Tycho is the author of several books, including *Inspirational Thoughts,* Y*ou are what you think* and *You really are responsible.* He is currently running his own publishing company - *Ocean Books.*

The British Centre for Wholistic Health situated in North London, offers various courses and workshops designed for attaining high level health and enhancing your personal growth and spiritual development. For more information, either phone or send a stamped addressed envelope to the address below:

The British Centre for Wholistic Health
18 Pentrich Avenue,
Enfield,
Middlesex EN1 4LZ.

Tel (0181) 350 9600

The National Society for Personal Growth.

This society exists primarily to link together like-minded people, for interesting meetings, discussions, and exchange of information about topics of mutual interest.

Some of the topics of interest include:
♦   Wholistic Health.
♦   Hypnosis.
♦   Homeopathy.
♦   Enhancing your immunity.
♦   Colon detoxification
♦   Possible cures for cancer and AIDS.
♦   Social and medical dogma.
♦   Religious and scientific dogma.
♦   Self-confidence and self-esteem.
♦   What is meditation?
♦   Finding inner peace.
♦   Realising your full potential.
♦   Goal setting.
♦   Self-empowerment and responsibility.
♦   The technique of self-suggestion.
♦   Trusting in life - learning to take risks.
♦   The power of the mind.
♦   The unity of all things.
♦   Tapping into inner wisdom.
♦   Learning from every experience.

Membership to the Society costs only £12 for 1 year. For this small fee, you will receive:

☞   A free 120 page book of inspirational quotations.

☞   Bi-monthly articles written by Tycho or Andrea.

☞ The opportunity to meet up with other local members.

☞ Information about courses and workshops offered at *The British Centre for Stress Management*.

☞ Gatherings of society members with the intention of meeting like-minded people and discussing topics of mutual interest.

☞ Occasional book reviews and the facility to exchange books with other society members.

We will circulate a list of members once or twice a year as required.

To become a society member or for more information phone (0181) 350 9600. Alternatively write to 18 Pentrich Avenue, Enfield, Middlesex. EN1 4LZ.